One More Victim

Books by A. M. Rosenthal

UN: Record and Prospects

Thirty-eight Witnesses

Books by Arthur Gelb

O'Neill

(WITH BARBARA GELB)

Bellevue Is My Home

(WITH BARBARA GELB & DR. SALVATORE CUTOLO)

Books Coedited
by A. M. Rosenthal and Arthur Gelb

The Pope's Journey to the United States

The Night the Lights Went Out

One More Victim

A. M. Rosenthal and Arthur Gelb

The New American Library

First Printing

Published by The New American Library, Inc.
1301 Avenue of the Americas, New York, New York 10019

Published simultaneously in Canada
by General Publishing Company, Ltd.

Library of Congress Catalog Card Number: 67-24795
Printed in the United States of America

The authors express their deep appreciation to the many people who helped them in the research of this book. Most of these people must remain anonymous because of the nature of their occupations—Federal, state, and municipal law-enforcement specialists, social workers, psychologists, and undercover workers devoting themselves to fighting the fringe Nazi groups in the United States.

From Irving Spiegel, a reporter of long experience and attainment on *The New York Times,* the authors received invaluable help and advice and we are particularly grateful to him. We also express our thanks to two other *Times* reporters who helped us in the research, Richard Reeves and Robert Dallos.

The authors wish to express their thanks for permission to quote from the following books: *Anti-Semite and Jew* by Jean-Paul Sartre, translated by George J. Becker. Copyright © 1948 by Schocken Books Inc. Reprinted by permission of Schocken Books Inc. *The Mind and Death of a Genius* by David Abrahamsen. Reprinted by permission of the author. *Portrait of a Jew* by Albert Memmi, © 1962, by the Orion Press, Inc. Reprinted by permission of the Orion Press, Inc.

To All the Other Victims

All things betray thee, who betrayest Me.

FRANCIS THOMPSON

One More Victim

Chapter One

On South Fourth Street, in Reading, a manufacturing town in a valley in southeastern Pennsylvania, there is a white shingle house with a vacant barber shop on the ground floor. It is quite an ordinary house, like a thousand others in Reading, but it is watched from time to time by the police of the city and its floor plan is noted in the dossiers of the Federal Bureau of Investigation.

One Sunday morning in October, 1965, a New Yorker named Daniel Burros, who was then twenty-eight years old, in excellent health, in love, and beginning to achieve status in the world in which he moved, which was the whole world to him, rushed into the house to the small bedroom behind the barber shop where he had been living for about a week, looked again at a headline on the front page of a copy of *The New York Times* that he was carrying, threw the newspaper on the floor, ran upstairs to his host's bedroom, tried to smash open a gun cabinet with karate kicks, saw a revolver lying on a bureau, seized it, and shot himself in the chest. He stood swaying for a moment, raised the gun again, sent a bullet into his left temple, and fell dead to the floor—all this from accounts told by three eyewitnesses to the Reading police.

When a man dies at twenty-eight, his years and achievements have been so few that they have touched on the lives of only a relatively small number of people, and it was so with Daniel Burros, a printer by trade. He was known, with bewilderment, to his parents and relatives, known with mild professional interest to a specialized group of policemen, known without much affection but with a small and growing degree of respect in a minute corner of American political life. At the time of his death, just a few hundred people had ever heard of Daniel Burros.

When a man dies at twenty-eight, his passing is noted hardly at all and is remembered and thought upon thereafter only by those who grieved for him, but it was not so with Daniel Burros. Few grieved for him—his mother and father, their brothers and sisters and children, perhaps two or three friends. But his death was known by millions, who heard about it on Sunday broadcasts or read about it in Monday's newspapers. There was shock, not so much over his death but over the revelation of his life. Among those who had become aware of him only when they heard of his death there was little sorrow, some rejoicing, more vengefulness, much disgust. But there was, most of all, among those who read or heard of the life and death of Daniel Burros, a sense that a mystery had been presented and that it had to do with how the soul of a man is corrupted.

Answers were sought that Sunday and Monday in homes throughout the country and later in churches and synagogues and in discussions among sociologists, psychiatrists, educators. The answers, of course, were shaped and determined by the beliefs and lives and experiences of those who gave them—the answer was in the warp of fear and hatred, the answer was in today's violence, the answer was in history, the answer was in good and evil, the answer was in the judgment of God.

The death of Daniel Burros did not answer the mystery

and it has not been answered yet. But it did raise questions, which at least is the first step in the search, the groping, for answers. And it did force men once again to peer into the tangible reality of hatred and of its meaning and its consequence.

Daniel Burros was a squat young man with watery blue eyes who wore his blond hair cut close. He walked with a rolling waddle and there were detectives in New York who called him "the Dwarf." He seemed put together awkwardly and gave the impression of dumpiness and being somehow off-center, but he was full-chested and strong-armed, and in repose his round face seemed gentle and about to smile.

Daniel Burros, who liked to read about philosophy, talk about politics, eat good food, and listen to Wagner, was a printer by trade and a killer by deep, unquenchable desire.

All his young adulthood Daniel Burros spent in the service of the far-right fringe in the United States. At his death he was King Kleagle of the New York Ku Klux Klan and before that he was an eager lieutenant in the tiny American Nazi movement. He shifted back and forth among the feuding splinter groups of the far right, from time to time forming his own. He made friends and he made enemies of friends quickly. Some of the American Nazis and KKK leaders saw him as a brilliant strategist and street gut-fighter, others as a mouthy braggart. But friends and enemies always knew and conceded that one thing nobody could take away from him—nobody hated the Jews more.

Membership in the far-right fringe and devotion to its service was not a goal for Burros but a means to an end—the death of the Jews. In this, he never wavered. He was a man whose enthusiasms sprang rapidly and withered rapidly, but the zest that filled him for the death and destruction of Jews, all Jews, never waned and for this he was known and admired in the world in which he moved.

It did happen sometimes that his enthusiasm for the extermination of the Jews embarrassed his comrades a little. In the shabby sweaty kind of barracks in Arlington where the handful of American Nazi "troopers" lived, the boys would look at each other and grin when Burros started talking about one of his daydreams—an instrument of torture, a piano whose wires, electrified, would be joined to the muscles and nerves of captive Jews. Funny idea all right, they would tell Burros, but stop talking about it when other people are around, kind of keep it in the family until the day comes.

Burros liked to draw and most of all he liked to draw pictures of Jews dead or dying. He had a mind for precise detail and most of all he was fascinated by the precise details of gas chambers. He was ambitious and most of all he was ambitious to be in charge of the extermination program. He liked uniforms and most of all the storm trooper's booted and belted uniform. He liked slogans and most of all he loved the simplest: "Kill."

He liked to write letters and he had a rubber-stamp swastika and a special way of signing off. *"Judah Verrecke,"* he would write with a flourish and sometimes provide his own translation—Perish Judah.

"The Jews must suffer and suffer," he liked to tell his friends and even they would sometimes get a little bored and tell him to turn it off for a while; then he would sulk.

He was a great collector, of insignia of German Army units and Nazi emblems, pictures of Hitler, photographs of the massacred and of the *Wehrmacht* in triumph. But he knew, and all who knew him knew, that "Perish Judah" was not a hobby for him but a life's goal, a work, a reason for being. He might bore his friends a bit, but they knew him for what he was—a man of single, entire dedication to what he wanted, the death of the Jew.

The Reading police conducted an investigation, issued a verdict of suicide. Some of the papers he carried on him—letters and membership cards in right-fringe groups—were filed at Reading police headquarters. But a little good-luck piece he liked to carry on him was never found. It was a small bar of soap labeled "From the finest Jewish fat."

Chapter Two

Sometimes, the elders of the Talmud Torah of Richmond Hill in the borough of Queens in New York used to tell each other that they could just lick their fingers about that boy. Not often these days, they would say, would a boy like Danny come along, so good, so sweet, so pious, so eager to study the Torah, such a student of Hebrew, such a fine example to other Jewish bar mitzvah boys in the neighborhood. Where could you find boys like that these days, particularly in a neighborhood where Saturdays were for stickball, not for the *schul?* He was like honey on the fingers.

The young rabbi of the congregation, Morris Appleman, agreed with the elders about Danny. It was Rabbi Appleman's first congregation and he was newly married. He was a round-faced, blue-eyed man, the son and the grandson of a rabbi, and his wife was also descended from a rabbinical family. Rabbi Appleman was a philosophical and a tolerant man, but it was not always easy to cope. The *schul* was in a predominantly Gentile neighborhood and the Jews who lived there didn't have much money to give to the new temple. There was competition from an older, established synagogue not far away. And it was difficult to deal tactfully with congregation members who liked to run his affairs.

Rabbi Appleman was pleased when the temple asked him to start a Hebrew school and assume personal charge of it;

the fees would be small, but they would help. It was hard, though, because there were few pupils, and those who came did so mostly under protest, regarding religious training as drudgery. They came for eight or nine months before their thirteenth birthdays to learn enough to fight their way through the bar mitzvah ceremony and then they escaped, like children on the last day of school.

But with Danny it was different. There was an exchange of gifts between the boy and the rabbi. The rabbi gave knowledge and the boy gave desire for knowledge. Every bar mitzvah boy studies from a *haftorah*—a small book in Hebrew and English that helps prepare him for the day he goes to the altar to read from the law for the first time. The books of all the other boys were scribbled with transliterations of the Hebrew to be used as crutches on the day of bar mitzvah. Danny's remained neat and clean and his was the only *haftorah* that Rabbi Appleman decided to keep. He kept it because he knew that Danny would amount to something—maybe a rabbi, maybe a professor, maybe something bigger, who knows? But surely Danny would amount to something and the rabbi would have his book always.

The rabbi knew Danny's mother, Esther, a small, quiet woman who would bring her twelve-year-old son by the hand to the synagogue because she was worried about the toughs in the neighborhood. He did not know Danny's father very well, because George Burros was a withdrawn, taciturn man who was not a temple-goer. But, without having to think about it, the rabbi knew what formed Danny's rhythm of life quite as much as his parents and his school and his friends and the streets he played on, because he knew where Danny "came from."

The rhythm of life built into an American Jewish child—the sound of the voices he hears about him, the stories he is told, the memories that are not really memories experienced but the talk of adults that become part of the child's past, his small prides and large fears, his picture of himself, as Jews and Christians see him, his sense of belonging or being outside, of being at ease or on edge—depends upon where he "comes from." And the answer determines how long he asks that question of himself, and how worried he is about it.

There is a world of nuance and a catalog of conditions that go into the answer; one condition plays on another, accents it or diminishes it, and only the total of the conditions, catalyzed, and all the shadings and subtleties produce the answer—one or another of the varieties of the American Jewish personality.

Both of Danny's grandfathers were Russian immigrants. Abraham Burros, father of George, was born in Vilna, emigrated to the United States in 1886, when he was twenty-one years old. Harry Sunshine, his wife, and their two-year-old daughter Esther arrived in the United States in 1904. These facts, recorded on the naturalization papers of Abraham Burros and Harry Sunshine when they renounced allegiance to Czar Nicholas II, emperor of all the Russias, were the structure on which Dan Burros' personality as an American Jew was built.

They meant that Dan was born into a slice of American life that had the taste and texture of eastern European Jewry. When Abraham Burros and Harry Sunshine arrived in New York (neither of them, when they filled out their naturalization papers, could remember the names of the ships that carried them and quite possibly never knew the names), they were as different from the Jews who had preceded them from other parts of the world in earlier waves of immigration as they were from the customs inspectors who waved them on.

The eastern European Jews who arrived in the United

States about the turn of the century were the greenhorns—not only to the American-born but to the immigrant Jews before them. They were removed totally from the aristocrats of American Jewish life, the Sephardic Jews who had arrived in the seventeenth century from Spain and Portugal, removed by the security of generations of settling.

They were removed almost as entirely from the German Jews who had arrived in the early part of the nineteenth century. The German Jews were trained and educated in Western ways, considered themselves Europeans as well as Jews—"up to date," the eastern Europeans would say with admiration—and although they knew the meaning of anti-Semitism, they lived within the protection of the law. Many of them arrived with money and with professions and most of all when they left they did not think themselves foreigners in Germany, which armed them against the inner tremble of people who consider themselves always foreigners, everywhere.

Abraham Burros and Harry Sunshine were Jews of a different kind. They came from the Russia where Jews by law were separate, where by tradition Jews were prey. Their fathers and their fathers before them knew that the Jew in Russia was a special kind of human being—the ordained, unprotected victim.

These were the tailors and the peddlers, the shoemakers of the old country and they became the tailors and the peddlers and the shoemakers of the new. Abraham Burros, on his naturalization papers, listed his trade as shoemaker. Harry Sunshine called himself a shoe dealer.

They came not just from Jewishness, but from Yiddishness. A German Jew speaks English with a German accent, a French Jew with a French accent. Abraham Burros and Harry Sunshine did not speak English with Russian accents, but with the particular cadence and lilt that is immediately recognizable as Yiddish—a mélange of medieval German, Hebrew, and eastern European languages. It was Yiddish, not Russian, that Russian Jews spoke among themselves because they were barred from Russian schools, forced to live only among Jews.

Their Yiddishness was not only a matter of accent. There is a Yiddish outlook, half-fearful, half-defiant. There is the quality of the mask to Yiddishness. Behind it are the terrors of fighting to survive, and behind it also a special humor, sharp and self-deprecating. But also behind the mask is a special pride that comes from the cherished realization that having fought to survive, and having won, is a matter of some worth, that other men and other people have either not survived or, having survived, have lost their ways.

Rabbi Appleman knew that Dan "came from" eastern European Yiddishness and that it would be part of him always, in the sudden flash memories of his grandparents and the way they walked and the way they moved their hands, their broken singsong English and the nervousness about the world that they took into steerage with them, as real as their bundles of bedding and clothes.

The rabbi knew too, again without having to think about it, that Dan "came from" other things, that he was a mixture but an understandable one. He was a Jew, a Jew of an eastern European background, and he was also a native-born Jew.

The process of dilution of Dan Burros' Yiddishness began the day Abraham Burros stepped off the boat. The single most important reality for every eastern European Jewish immigrant was that no matter what men thought of him, the law no longer set him aside. Many things did set him aside—language and newness and tradition and appearance and fear, but not the law.

The "Golden Land," the Yiddish Jews called America and often, suffocated by tenement, sweaty with labor, and bitter with "kike" in their ears, they said it like an oath. "A curse on Christopher Columbus," they would mutter to each other. At least in the old country a man could breathe the air and if he was a kike, he was a kike among kikes, not among ignoramuses, and how sweet were the strawberries they ate in their youth.

The bitternesses and the failures and the homesickness were real, but the Yiddish Jews knew that their lives were forever different, not just because they lived within the protection of the law but because their children and their children's children would live within it. They saw their children and their children's children change in appearance from the Jewish children they knew in the old country. They stuffed them with milk and meat and they shook their heads with sheer delight at the sight of a twelve-year-old stronger and bigger than his father or his uncle, and when they did not curse Christopher Columbus they blessed him for producing young Jewish boys "strong as Cossacks."

Men like Abraham Burros knew that back home there had been big Jews, too, but that when the pogroms came they bled and no matter how tall they grew they could not climb the ghetto walls because strength comes not from sinew and inches but only from the law. Judaism is a law-based religion and the old Jews from eastern Europe knew also the supreme relevance of the protection of the law of man, knew it in the special way a wanderer in the winter knows the importance of a fire's warmth and the hungry man knows the value of bread.

Work was hard in the new country and there was no gold in the streets, but no Jew dreamt of returning. In the old countries, new governments might change the laws from time to time and tell their Jews not to worry, a new time was at hand, but the Jews of eastern Europe never believed, because they knew that hunters never put aside their guns. They trusted the law of the new land, because it had not smelled the blood of Jews ever, and their native-born children were not only beneficiaries of the laws of America but, by birthright, proprietors of it. The children were to the fathers as landowners to squatters. That was the essential difference, and the immigrant Jews drew pleasure and an additional sense of safety from their children's richness.

The tremulous rhythm of eastern European Yiddishness was part of Dan Burros' background. It was strengthened by the more secure beat of the American birthright and it took on the special cadence of poverty and New York. Dan was eastern European, American-born, and lived most of his life in a flat in a dingy building in Queens, and he "came from" no single one of these things, but from all.

As a young child, Dan seemed to accept where he "came from" simply as part of the life around him. His paternal grandfather, Abraham Burros, would sometimes bring him to his synagogue in South Ozone Park, the Sons of Israel Temple that he helped to found, and the other elders would smile to each other in approval. "A nice, juicy little boy," they called Dan, and they could see, from his shy and serious manner, that he would be pious, just like his grandfather. They expected him to be bar-mitzvahed in their synagogue; this was a matter of moment in a small congregation where each participating family is known and counted. Families move and slip away; there are feuds sometimes within a synagogue and that means losses. If a boy is bar-mitzvahed in a synagogue, the hope is that he and his family will develop allegiances to it, give strength to the congregation.

But Abraham Burros died in 1948, when Dan was eleven.

Dan's father was not a member of the Sons of Israel—not, in fact, much of a temple-goer at all—and Mrs. Burros decided to enroll Dan for his bar mitzvah instruction in the Congregation Talmud Torah, the new Orthodox synagogue at 109–25 114th Street, in Richmond Hill, less than a half mile from the Sons of Israel in Ozone Park.

Every adult practicing Jewish male is a bar mitzvah, a phrase translated by scholars of Judaism as "man of duty" or "son of the commandment." The ceremony of bar mitzvah is probably a relic of tribal initiation—the acceptance of a boy of puberty, not into the tribe, for he was born into it, but into the responsibilities and privileges of tribal membership.

It used to be, not simply in antiquity but within the memories of men like Abraham Burros, that at thirteen childhood was left behind. A boy became a man, a man who would work and take on his responsibility to his family, his community, and as a witness in his religion.

But age was not enough to be granted the rights of adulthood within the religious society. A boy had to be taught the fundamentals of his religion, the meaning of the law, the ritual and ceremony of worship. In antiquity this was the father's duty. Until the boy was thirteen, the father was responsible for his son's moral and religious health. At thirteen, the boy stood on his own and the father, recognizing this, said a prayer of gratitude in the synagogue: "Blessed be He Who has taken from me the responsibility for this boy."

It was some time in the Middle Ages that the bar mitzvah ceremony came to include not just the father and son and rabbi but the entire community of the synagogue. It became something more than a step into religious adulthood. It became a demonstration of ability to accept adulthood, to understand and to think. It is not an act of salvation or grace or acceptance of belief but of satisfactory fulfillment of tests of knowledge, rather like a diploma.

In the ghetto days, by the time a Jewish boy was thirteen he had been steeped in Judaism and his entry into religious adulthood was a reality, not a symbol. He was not trained specifically for the bar mitzvah ceremony—the reading of the weekly portion of the Torah nearest to his birth date and the selection from the prophetic books of the Bible—but was able to perform the ceremony merely as a demonstration of a small part of his scholarship.

Once a bar mitzvah he was a full member of the congregation, not a junior. He was counted as part of the *minyan,* the quorum of ten needed for worship in a synagogue. He could be counted as among the quorum of three for the recitation of grace after meals. And before morning prayers, an automatic part of his life became the wearing of *tefillin* as the outward reminder of his Jewish identity and his personal commitment to the Torah—two individual small boxes, each containing two passages on parchment from Exodus and Deuteronomy, attached to two leather thongs, one wrapped around the left arm, the other around the forehead. "God also wears *tefillin,*" the old Jews used to say.

"Today I am a man," bar mitzvah boys said in the ghetto and meant it and knew their elders considered them men. In the New World, Jewish boys were bigger and broader than the ghetto boys, but they were not men because they were not forced by the need of their labor into early manhood. Neither they nor the congregation considered them men except in the religious sense and inevitably the fact that they were not considered men of the community came to change the significance of the bar mitzvah ceremony, from entry to adulthood, into a symbol of entry.

The entire pattern of religious life for Jewish boys, even

those from devout households, changed. In the ghetto, the lives of men were immersed in religion and the synagogue and so were the lives of their sons. Judaism was not part-time but total, total religious observance at home, total in the synagogue, the totality and goal of education. There was only one subject fit for a man's study—the Torah and the Talmudic commentary on the law derived from the Torah, that great library of sixty-three volumes developed over centuries, each volume itself the subject of examination, and volumes of dissertation. (What is the Torah, a pagan demanded of the sage Hillel and challenged him to tell him its essence while the pagan stood on one foot. Hillel said: "What is hateful to you, do not do to your neighbor. This is the entire Torah. The rest is commentary thereon. . . . Go, study!")

In the New World, the synagogue became for most Jews something for Saturdays and the holidays. The morning prayers at home began to disappear from most Jewish households. Youngsters were educated in English in public schools, not in Hebrew in synagogue schools, and the purpose of education was not to make a boy a scholar in his religion but to equip him to understand and compete in the world.

But almost every Jew in the New World held to the ceremony of bar mitzvah for his boys. It came to mean not real adulthood, but the passing on of a heritage from father to son. And as the ritual richness of the heritage became more strained, and the day-to-day quality of Judaism became in many households more attenuated, Jewish parents reached out more, rather than less, to the bar mitzvah. Fathers who did not go to synagogue from one Yom Kippur to the other insisted on the bar mitzvah for their sons because they felt that without the bar mitzvah ceremony there was no participation in Jewish communal life. Not to be bar-mitzvahed was to accept being alone.

The nature of the bar mitzvah changed, particularly among American Jews with a little money. The ceremony itself became a prelude to gift-giving—"Today I am a fountain pen," Jewish boys say—and for a party that often was a testimonial to the parents from the parents. The nature of acceptance into religious adulthood changed, too; bar mitzvah boys often consider the ceremony an end to their religious obligations, instead of a beginning, and nobody really expects them to present themselves for daily prayer at the synagogue. There are synagogues where those boys who do attend after bar mitzvah are shunted off to *minyans* in "junior congregations."

And the Jewish education of boys became not the total of their schooling, but a kind of cram course for the bar mitzvah day. The rabbi's hope is to draw the students into a love of Jewish learning that will continue after bar mitzvah day; more pragmatically his immediate objective is to stuff enough knowledge into their heads so that they won't make fools of themselves and of him when they first stand up to read from the Torah—"If they can't understand the words, at least let them know how to pronounce them." The boys attend a couple of hours after school because their parents insist on it and bar mitzvah day is regarded as a kind of an end to an obstacle course, to be rewarded with a big party.

The Talmud Torah of Richmond Hill was built of brick and shaped like a squared-off Quonset hut. But it was about the same size as the one-family houses around it and melded unobtrusively into the street.

From his home, Dan walked past his old school, P.S. 100, past the imposing Our Lady of Perpetual Help Roman Catholic Church and parochial school, down a street of maple trees to the small congregation schoolhouse next to the synagogue. His mother walked with him. The classroom was on the right, across the vestibule—four rows of desk arm chairs, five abreast.

The first time Rabbi Appleman saw Mrs. Burros was when she came to enroll Danny. He was in the synagogue itself then, had entered the rear door most people used. The door led into a kind of kitchen-reception room—a sink, a refrigerator, a long table where cake and wine were placed after services and where parents laid out a spread after bar mitzvahs. The synagogue was a simple room, with space for about one hundred fifty folding chairs, a waist-high board wall running down the middle to separate the women from the men.

The rabbi remembers Mrs. Burros saying that she wanted "a little Jewishness" for her son, an education for bar mitzvah. Her husband was not very interested in such things, she said, so it was up to her. She was worried about the cost—at the Sons of Israel parents had to join the temple if they wanted their sons to go to Hebrew school, and that cost money.

At the Talmud Torah, there was no such requirement. The rabbi was allowed to run the Hebrew school himself, as an adjunct to his salary of one hundred dollars a month, and so he made arrangements with Mrs. Burros—a dollar a week.

Danny started his lessons in the late fall of 1949 and he came, the rabbi says, "like a clock, the ticking of a clock." He had a way of looking down in bashfulness and he seemed a little embarrassed to have his mother walk him to the Hebrew school; he was, after all, twelve years old. The rabbi and his wife always thought of Dan and his mother as inseparable.

The only writing in Dan Burros' *haftorah* was the name printed on the inside back cover. Dan learned first the Hebrew alphabet, then the passage from the Torah that was to be the passage for the Sabbath on the day he was to be bar-mitzvahed, March 4 or the fifteenth day of Adar in the Hebrew calendar—Genesis 30: Verses 8, 9, and 10—and his *haftorah,* the portion from the prophets assigned as supplement to the week's Torah reading. His passage was from Ezekiel, Chapter 43, and dealt with Ezekiel's exhortation to the Jews, after the destruction of the First Temple in Jerusalem, that they repent their sins if they wanted to rebuild the Temple.

> Thou son of man, show the house to the house of Israel that they may be ashamed of their iniquities and let them measure the pattern.
>
> And if they be ashamed of all that they have done, show them the form of the house and the fashion thereof, and the goings out thereof, and the comings in thereof, and all the forms thereof, and all the ordinances thereof, and all the forms thereof, and all the laws thereof, and write it in their sight, that they may keep the whole form thereof, and all the ordinances thereof, and do them.

The rabbi and his wife were drawn to Dan; they put it down to his studiousness and his sweetness of nature, and on Friday nights often would invite him to dinner. The rabbi would ask Dan what he wanted to be and Dan would talk about being an artist, and the rabbi would drop a word or two about the rabbinate.

Once the rabbi was talking to Mrs. Burros about an emblem he wanted drawn for the school, a picture of an old man with his hand around the shoulder of a boy and around the rim the words: "And I shall teach them diligently unto thy children." Mrs. Burros said her Danny could do it and volunteered for him. Dan did draw it and the rabbi used it for the front page of his bulletin and kept it, along with Dan's *haftorah.*

On the day of bar mitzvah, Dan's mother and father came

and so did other relatives, and the rabbi was proud. Dan read beautifully and afterward there was cake and wine for everybody, brought by Mrs. Burros. There was no big bar mitzvah party, no huge "catered affair" that American Jews with money love to give. But the next day the rabbi and his wife were invited to Dan's home for a little spread—cold cuts and soda—and Dan greeted them "like a king and a queen." There was more life in his face than they had seen before and everybody laughed and talked a lot. George Burros, quiet as usual, said little more than "hello" to the rabbi and his wife.

The real joy for the rabbi and the elders came after Dan's bar mitzvah. Most of the boys in his bar mitzvah class dropped away, or came only on holidays with their parents, but Dan came almost every day to morning prayers and the old Jews loved to look upon his face in prayer, and so did the rabbi. On Yom Kippur, Dan came to synagogue—the rabbi had given him a free ticket. (It is at the time of the high holidays that congregations earn most of their money for the year through the sale of tickets.) He was dressed entirely in white, white shirt, white trousers, even white sneakers instead of shoes. He did as the Jews of antiquity, on the day of atonement, and clothed himself in the color of purification. And Dan continued to come to the temple on Saturday afternoons, when Mrs. Appleman led a small group of boys and girls in the study of the Talmud. Dan seemed always the most eager of the group to learn. After reading and discussing a section of the Talmud, the children would sometimes sing Israeli songs and learn Israeli dances.

Dan's relationship with the temple and with Rabbi Appleman and his wife continued for about eight months after his bar mitzvah. Then the rabbi was offered a larger congregation on Long Island and he accepted because he needed more money for his family, which now included a baby. Word got around the neighborhood that the rabbi would be leaving soon and a change came over Dan. He went to the temple less often and when he did go the rabbi noticed he was more quiet than usual—even a little bit sullen.

Rabbi Appleman believed that Dan's affinity for Judaism was very much a part of Dan's personal affection for him. The rabbi tried to talk to Dan, to explain the reason for his leaving, but Dan did not seem to respond. Rabbi Appleman vaguely feared that Dan regarded his leaving as a kind of betrayal. But he felt sure that Dan would get over his hurt.

Rabbi Appleman believed in Dan, believed he would be a somebody, and was convinced that the little chubby boy with the blond hair and blue eyes and kindly ways was and would always be, a son of the commandment, a man of duty.

Chapter Three

Lloyd Contract and a few of the other neighborhood boys from John Adams High School were playing stickball in the yard of P.S. 100, as they often did on a fall Saturday morning, when Lloyd's friend started the argument. It was the same old argument that Lloyd's friend always started, about World War II, and about how Germany had been right, how Germany had been misunderstood. Lloyd had heard it time and again from his friend, had been to his house and seen the pictures of Rommel on the wall, and the pictures of German planes and tanks hanging over his bed, had seen his friend's Iron Cross. He had heard his friend say that the only way to save America was with a gun, that anybody who thought otherwise was un-American. He had listened to him talk of his plans, talk eternally of his plans to go to West Point and rise in the Army.

Lloyd was a studious boy with a bent for engineering. He was a Jew and he was repelled by his friend's constant talk of Germany and his worship of the German generals. But the subject of religion never came up and nothing anti-Semitic was ever said, so although the friendship became frayed it did not break until that Saturday in 1954, after they had known each other for five years and they were both juniors at John Adams in Queens.

It was a cloudy, drizzly day, still warm enough for light

zipper-jackets. Again, Lloyd's friend started talking about the injustice done to Germany. He drew himself up to his full height of five feet seven inches, assuming his version of a military stance, as he always did during arguments, puffed out his face, screamed, banged his right fist into his left hand. Lloyd and his friend shouted back and forth. Lloyd called him an idiot. Suddenly the friend struck, twice to the body. Lloyd pushed hard, cornered his friend against the school gate.

"Jew bastard," Dan Burros shouted at Lloyd. There was a quick silence; the two boys looked at each other, parted, and never spoke again.

In Richmond Hill, stationery stores sold little cardboard kaleidoscopes for a dime. You held them to your eye and through a glass saw the colored pieces of celluloid fall into a pattern. If you turned the toy in your hands the pieces fell into an entirely different pattern. Each pattern was true or real, although no beholder ever saw the same pattern, because each pattern was composed of all the pieces. It happened sometimes that the pieces would stick together, blue over yellow, and then green was real. Sometimes boys would trade kaleidoscopes with each other, because they were all a little different—different numbers of pieces, different colors, different shapes. The fun of it, of course, was that two people could not look through the eyepiece at the same time, so no two boys could ever see the same thing at the same time, know exactly what the other boy saw, and it was delightfully tantalizing. Sometimes a toy would break and the pattern become frozen. Or it would become a bore and be thrown away, landing in a closet or a drawer or the gutter and falling into one final arrangement of colored celluloid bits that no boy would ever see.

There were four years from the day of Ezekiel to the day of "Jew bastard," but the flight did not begin in the Congregation Talmud Torah any more than it ended in the schoolyard of P.S. 100. It did not begin at any moment in time that can be isolated; the pieces of the kaleidoscope were present when Dan was seen through the eyes of Rabbi Appleman and the elders and they were present when Lloyd saw him in the schoolyard.

The difference between Dan and the kaleidoscope, of course, is that in the boy the pieces were related to one another always and intrinsically, not occasionally as in blue over yellow, and that one pattern shaped the following. At any moment, a kaleidoscope can be torn apart, each piece separated and examined. The pieces that formed the final design within Dan Burros exist now as reflections and shadows, memories and guilts, love and repugnance, but all these things are born of specific events—known as "reality"—and, therefore, insofar as they can be traced and isolated, are quite real still.

Some of the truth of Dan Burros is not known because most of those few people who loved him seek surcease from their anguish and can find no release yet and are not ready for the catharsis of resurrected pain. But enough is known, in the reality of memoirs of others, or in what Dan Burros revealed of himself, to show that the boy who shouted "Jew bastard" lived in the boy who read from Ezekiel and to conjecture how one came to conquer the other.

Dan was the only child of parents who married late in life. Esther Sunshine was thirty-four and lived with her parents in a Bronx apartment when she married George Burros. George, forty-two, worked intermittently as a machinist. Although a quiet youth, he had been an adventurous one and he had paid a price for his adventures. He had joined the Navy before World War I when he was about sixteen. At the end of his enlistment term he switched to the Army and found himself with the First Division pursuing Pancho Villa. Still an enlisted man when the United States entered World War I, he was shipped to France, where he received a throat wound that severely damaged his vocal chords and impaired his speech. His wound made him even more introverted than he had been before his enlistment.

George and Esther were married on May 31, 1936. The marriage was performed by a rabbi in a small hired hall in the Bronx. George, whose bouts of ill health prevented his holding a steady job, depended mainly on his Government pension, and Esther worked as a saleswoman from time to time after their marriage.

Dan was born in Lebanon Hospital in the Bronx on March 5, 1937, and shortly thereafter George and Esther moved to Richmond Hill to be near George's family; for the next ten years they blended into the patriarchal household of Abraham Burros.

Abraham Burros, who had spent much of his life wandering, had finally put down his roots in the Richmond Hill area when he was in his sixties, and retired. He and his wife, Anna Yolke, a Vilna girl, had raised six sons and four daughters, several of whom lived with them in Queens. Abraham was among the immigrant Jews who left New York City soon after they arrived in the United States. (His original Russian-Yiddish patronymic was written down phonetically by an immigration officer and came out as "Burros.") The usual reason was that friends or relatives were settled elsewhere and offered them jobs or prospects of jobs, or at least a home while they looked, a home and the comfort of familiar faces from the old country. Abraham had a brother who had settled in Waterbury, Connecticut.

Three years after Abraham got off the boat, his first son, Jacob, was born in Meriden, Connecticut. The family lived in and around Bridgeport as the sons and daughters grew. They left Connecticut for Long Island City in Queens, where George, Dan's father, was born, and a year later they returned to Connecticut. The last child, Solomon Gershon, was born in 1909.

When Abraham settled into his final home in Richmond Hill, he was surrounded by children, friends, and love.

One of Abraham's sons, Joseph, was a New York City policeman—a somewhat unusual occupation for a Jew of that background and time. Eleven years George's junior, Joe had joined the police force at twenty-eight, after having worked as a bookkeeper. Danny admired his Uncle Joe and loved to hear stories about the police force. He also listened to his father's tales of his war experiences; in the sympathetic atmosphere of Abraham's household, George Burros lost his shyness and would talk for hours about his adventures in the Army and Navy. He and Danny built model ships together and he encouraged Danny to pore over the books he had about naval history. George Burros seemed content to let Danny absorb his sense of Jewishness from Abraham.

When Abraham's wife died of cancer in 1942—Dan was five years old then—the grandfather took over the running of the household, even to the cooking and baking. At Passover, there would be huge family feasts, with friends swelling the company to forty or fifty.

The family gatherings stopped, except for special occasions like a wedding or a funeral, when Abraham died. Dan, then eleven, and his parents seemed, to Abraham's old friends in the Sons of Israel Congregation, to withdraw into themselves.

Abraham's friends used to see George once in a while, in the streets, but George liked his privacy and usually there was not more than a word or two—hello and good-bye, not the kind of man you talk things over with.

They didn't talk things over and there was no bond between the elders and George's family. But in a neighborhood like Richmond Hill and in a synagogue like Sons of Israel people know what's going on—"Don't ask me how we know," they say, "we know; we have eyes and ears."

The eyes told them that things were not going too well with George and his family. Richmond Hill was a neighborhood mostly of one- and two-family houses, and the Burros lived in one of the few apartment buildings, and one of the shabbiest.

It was a two-story, yellow brick building with a high front stoop, divided into four apartments. The Burros lived in one of the rear apartments, up a flight of narrow wooden stairs. There was only one bedroom—Dan's—that opened off a hallway. A door at the end of the hall led to the kitchen and there was a living room where George and Esther slept.

The Lefferts Boulevard apartment house was a building left behind. Growing up around it were new brick houses, with little gardens. The new people in the new houses were annoyed with the old house; it didn't look nice, they said; it should be torn down.

Across the street was a small bar—beer and rye were the big sellers—and diagonally across was Bohack's. Esther Burros used to shop here and on Saturdays Dan would help her, carrying back the deposit bottles. On the sidewalk outside the building was a United States Army recruiting poster on an iron stand that the neighborhood kids swung on and moved up and down the block as a prank.

Richmond Hill, when Dan grew up there, was—and still

is—small town New York. The eye is brought down in Richmond Hill because the houses are small, two- or three-story brick houses, one-story shops that service householders—the signs say plumbing, gas, window shades. There is a faintly seedy rundown quality to the neighborhood as if the people who lived in it had grown tired—not careless but tired. The lawns are neatly kept, but the street pavements are cracking a little and the city does not rush to repair them. It is a neighborhood that has not decayed or become a slum, it just has faded a bit because the people who live in it have neither money power nor minority power. The people who live in it are the lifetime middle class; they haven't come terribly far and they aren't going very far and if the city has forgotten them, they prefer it that way.

Once, Richmond Hill was an attainment. Between the tenements of the Lower East Side and the "fresh air" neighborhoods where men like Abraham Burros moved, there were decades of labor. The turn-of-the-century immigrants used to dream of places like Richmond Hill—not too fancy to be frightening, not too expensive to be unreachable, not too native American to be uncomfortable, but a place where a man could find a nice little house and nice maple trees in the streets, almost like the country, but still not too far from Manhattan's work.

To move into a neighborhood like Richmond Hill, an eastern European Jew needed a sense of adventure and a little courage. There are Jewish neighborhoods in New York and there are neighborhoods that were Christian and took on a Jewish flavor when Jews moved in. Richmond Hill is one of those neighborhoods that retained its own, non-Jewish identity, where Jews came, moved out, were replaced by Jews and non-Jews; it was never dominated by any sense of stranger's takeover. There were never enough Jews for the Jewish shopkeepers to move in, in any important number, and it is the Jewish shops and the shops that cater to Jews that give a neighborhood a Jewish quality. When Jews say "this is not a Jewish neighborhood," they are not talking just about census counts but about candy stores and dry goods stores and kosher delicatessens and Chinese restaurants. Even the chains of supermarkets tell a Jew what the neighborhood is like, a "Daitch" sign means a Jewish neighborhood, "Bohack's" usually means a bagle-less desert.

The houses Dan saw every day, the streets he walked to school and what he saw along them and what he heard, the kind of stores he shopped in for his mother, were the realities of his days and the texture of his life. Every New York boy lives on an island within a city. Behind him and all around him, but as a kind of backdrop, is the totality of New York—crowds in a subway, black people dimly perceived or white people dimly perceived, downtown where offices are and money is earned and department stores visited on occasional Saturdays, the treat places like Coney Island, the museums where you look and shove, the Radio City Music Hall, girls in the *Daily News,* menus in restaurants, nickles to spend in the Automat. All these things become familiar because they are seen, heard, smelled, so often. They are off-island and, therefore, even in proximity set apart. The island, center stage, center life, where things really happen and are important, is the neighborhood.

Dan entered kindergarten in P.S. 100 and until he finished sixth grade and was transferred to another school, Mrs. Burros walked with him most mornings to the gate, a half-block from the house. When school was over, she was waiting for him to take him home and give him a bite to eat to tide him over to supper time.

One of Dan's friends in the early grades was Clarence

Anspake, and Clarence's mother liked to have Dan visit the house. He spoke so softly and seemed to play so well with Clarence and he had such good manners—if a grown-up came in he always jumped up and if he was offered a Coke he would always look to see if Clarence was having one, too, so it wouldn't be too much trouble. When it got dark, Mrs. Burros would come over to take Danny home and she would chat a little. Once, Mr. Burros came over, but he just waited with his coat on and said no, thank you, he wouldn't come in for a while. Mrs. Burros was in the hospital that day and Danny wasn't allowed to go home at the usual time, about six or seven, but had to wait until Mr. Burros showed up at about nine in the evening.

Sometimes, Clarence would visit Dan on Friday nights, when they could stay up a little later because there was no school the next day. Mrs. Burros asked Mrs. Anspake to send Clarence over because, she said, Dan didn't have many friends.

At P.S. 100 Dan was one of the little boys who make the lives of schoolteachers easy—obedient, never late, well behaved, bright. He was a B-plus boy, an A boy, with a flair for drawing and a fine reader—two years and more above his grade level.

P.S. 100 only went up to the sixth grade and when they finished that Dan and Clarence and their whole class were transferred to P.S. 121, an eight-grade school nearby, to complete the last two grades before high school.

There are hundreds of schools like 100 and 121 in New York, and in the new school Dan found the comfort of familiarity. A solid, red brick building, with about fifteen hundred students, thirty-five to forty in a class. A no-nonsense building with the only touch of grandeur the marble stairway leading to the principal's office, a stairway children usually do not use. Before school and during recess, he ran about in the play area that had a prison-yard atmosphere. The children could yell and race in the yard; monitors kept an eye on the gates to make sure nobody strayed into the dangers of the street. Inside the school corridors, Dan and the other children talked in whispers lest they "get reported."

The children ate their lunches in a lunchroom that seemed forever to smell of orange peel. Dan's classrooms in the seventh and eighth grade were on the fifth floor of the school—too far for the smaller children to climb. As he entered the class he would make for the wardrobe in the rear, where the children hung their coats. Each room had an American flag in front and at the start of each day the children pledged allegiance to the flag and sang "The Star-Spangled Banner."

The rooms were bright, with large windows, and in the rear were exhibits of pictures that showed excursions taken by the class, or special projects of the children. They sat at old wooden school desks screwed to the floor, with a hole in the upper right-hand corner, where inkwells used to be. Dan and all the other children used ball-point pens and the wells remained dry. Names and initials were carved on the desks, and a few swastikas.

Dan never "got reported," never had any trouble, earned a 92 average in the seventh grade, a 93 in the eighth, an "all around good kid" to teachers who no longer remember him but see him through the kaleidoscope of marks on school records.

An "all around good kid" to his public school teachers and, during this same period, "the *machiah*"—deliciousness—and "the prayer" to some of the elders of the Talmud Torah. To Rabbi Appleman the shy bar mitzvah boy who would grow up to personify the virtues of Jewishness.

Only to one or two of Dan's schoolmates—never to an adult

—was there a hint of something unstable, something too intense, in Dan's makeup. A boy who attended both Hebrew school and public school with Dan has recalled being somewhat puzzled by "Dan's ardent religiosity." The boy, who grew up to be a rabbi and will here be called Saul, regarded Dan's religious devotion as "abnormal"; as far as Saul could see, Dan had no religious friends and did not have the kind of absorption with religion in his daily life that supported the fervor he displayed at the Talmud classes. Saul's feeling about Dan was confirmed on the Yom Kippur following the one on which Dan had attended synagogue dressed all in white. Saul met Dan on the street that Yom Kippur morning.

"He was carrying his books, and was on his way to school," Saul has recalled. "Even the least religious Jewish child stays out of school on Yom Kippur. Dan was probably the only Jew in school that day." (Much later, Dan himself was to maintain that his childhood absorption with the rituals of Judaism had been imposed upon him by his family—that he had been "pressured" into the bar mitzvah.)

Dan brought the same kind of intensity—the furious all-or-nothing approach that he had for religion—to other activities. Clarence Anspake was Dan's favorite chess partner in the seventh and eighth grades. Clarence was stunned at the way Dan played.

As the game wore on, Dan would break into sweat at the approaching victory or defeat, and if he thought he were losing, would keep the game going for three or four hours more, as long as Clarence would stand for it, fighting desperately for a stalemate. He did not say much if he lost, which was not often, but if he won he would laugh, high and loud, with glee.

It was the same way with the boat in the seventh grade and the dancing class in the eighth. Everybody was building a model boat in shop class, a sailboat. Most of the boys built boats about two feet long. As soon as Dan saw that two feet was to be the average length, he built one four feet long.

Nobody liked the dancing class; like all the other boys Dan was at that age studiously, determinedly contemptuous of girls and dancing. But the teachers were determined to pound a little grace into the boys and girls and marched them into the gym for the class. The boys stood on one side, the girls on the other, giggling. "Choose a partner, choose a partner," the teacher commanded and nobody did. A grim-faced Dan finally stepped forward, picked out a little dark-haired girl and stomped around the floor with her, the couple alone, until the music stopped and he returned to the boys' side of the room in triumph.

In the schoolyard of 121 and in the streets of Richmond Hill, Dan was "soldier boy" and the kid with the quick fists who was so funny in his fury when he fought that it was as good as a show.

Dan looked for fights, relished them, even when he took a beating. At P.S. 121 one day, in the yard, Dan looked around, found the biggest boy there, began shoving. The fight lasted about ten minutes, with fifteen boys crowding around, rooting this time for Dan because he was the little one, the underdog. The underdog lost and went home with a bloody nose and a bloody mouth, but he seemed happy to Clarence. He said to Clarence, so what if he lost, if he had won it would have shown who was who around there, and, anyway, he was somebody who would stand out because didn't he have the guts to pick on a kid twice as big?

Sometimes he walked home with Ronald Moloff and almost every day there was a fight; it was almost like a ritual between the two boys. Dan would start an argument—about the St. Louis Cardinals, often, because they were his favorite team, and most boys in the neighborhood liked the home town teams, the Giants or the Yankees or the Dodgers. Ronald would hit for the mouth, and the braces over Dan's teeth would break. Dan would jump up and down—his "banzai" charge he liked to call it—and scream, "I'm going to kill you." Then the fight would be over and Dan, picking nervously at his lip, would confide some more about his love for the Cards and urge Ronald not to tell anybody that he had a Cardinal scrapbook because the other guys in the neighborhood might beat him up for not supporting the New York team. The next day, another fight about something else. Dan never would give up. If Ronald hit him and decided he had won, Dan would run after him to fight some more. Sometimes Ronald would go home crying, Dan never.

When they were in the eighth grade one day the two boys were down on the sidewalk fighting and Ronald was banging Dan's head into the ground; a woman pulled them apart, both boys in a total rage. Later Mrs. Burros went in search of Ronald and told him to stay away from her boy—"You're a bad influence on him."

(Ronald is a dentist now, practicing in Westchester. "The more I think of it, the chances are I probably needled him more than he needled me. But I can't remember why.")

Most of Dan's friends remember him fighting; a few remember him always up or down, black or white, everything wonderful or everything terrible. At punchball, if somebody made a good catch, Dan would jump up and down and scream his joy. If somebody dropped a fly ball, there would be a tantrum from Dan—"Calm down, screwloose," the boys would say.

"Honey on the fingers" at the Congregation Talmud Torah—and "soldier boy" or "you, General" or "Here comes West Point" in the streets. Lots of boys fought, lots of boys had tempers and although they didn't fight or scream as much as Dan, still temper and fists were not enough to mark him in the neighborhood, to fix his pattern in the minds of his friends. Soldiering was.

Dan liked to tell his friends, listen you had to be tough—and listen, soldiers were plenty tough and they can keep people in line and it's West Point for me, you know my father got medals in the war and he's American Legion, you know, and I am going to be a cadet; wait.

You? West Point? Some of his friends were simply astonished at the idea because, a Jewish boy—West Point? Others liked to get him to talk about it, nodding seriously until he got wide-eyed with enthusiasm and then they would scream with laughter. Fatso the general, the West Pointer with glasses, Colonel Cohen. Danny—what are you going to do with your braces when you blow your bugle, Danny. Go boomboom, Danny, make like a machine gun. Sometimes they mocked him just because the idea was so funny, sometimes just because it was a good way to get the show started, to get Danny screaming with rage, to see his face grow red as a turkey and to watch him start flailing, his eyes teared with rage, until they pinned him down, socked him a little, and said, "Here's a medal for you, boomboom." Sometimes when they saw him they would shout "Attention!" and salute, thumb to nose.

But soldiers did salute Danny; proper salutes from the proper soldiers he loved to draw. He drew them at home and he drew them in his notebooks in school and on pieces of scratch paper, all kinds of soldiers. He pored over copies of "Prince Valiant" comic books and drew huge knights in huge castles. For Rabbi Appleman and his mother he drew the picture of the old man of wisdom leading the child to learning; for himself he drew pictures of young men of power leading armies to battle. Ronald Moloff's father had books of World War I and II pictures, and Danny would come to the house to pore over them, to study the details of uniforms and weapons.

Sometimes he would tell his friends that he drew soldiers as part of his "training" to go to West Point. Sometimes he would say that studying pictures of soldiers and war, and drawing pictures of uniformed men, just made him feel good.

There was a certain amount of neighborhood anti-Semitism that Dan heard about him—every Jewish boy growing up in a mixed Jewish and Gentile neighborhood in New York hears "Jew boy" and "Ikey." He says "Guinea bastard" or "Dirty mick" back, if he is big enough to get away with it or strong enough to fight, or turns away if he is not. He knows what blocks and what street corners he is most likely to hear it on, and Jewish boys have their own neighborhood safety maps in their minds, always.

In a strange way, most of the "Jew boy" epithets in Richmond Hill were almost complimentary—from peer to peer. The boys who heard them most were the Jewish boys strong enough and tough enough to play ball with the Italian and Irish boys in the public school yards or at Our Lady of Perpetual Help. These were the Jewish boys the Christian boys knew, and to be called "Ikey" during a ball game at least meant that you had pushed your way into the ball game and that you had been accepted, if not as part of the group, at least good enough at ball to stick around and pay the price of hazing.

Dan heard the "Jew boy" calls sometimes, but there is nobody who remembered him getting into a fight about anti-Semitism. But he remembered them and he also remembered that most of the Jewish boys preferred to avoid the bait rather than get into a fight. ("After a while," Ronald Moloff was to say, "when a couple of guys rap you in the mouth because you're Jewish, you don't yell out you're Jewish next time.")

Dan was never part of the accepted gang of Jewish and Christian ballplayers—too small, and not good enough. The fights he had were with Jewish boys and the taunts and derision about his dreams of soldiering were all from Jewish boys.

In neighborhoods like Richmond Hill, Jewish boys almost always know who the other Jewish boys are; there's a banding together. Some of Dan's friends knew he was Jewish and to one or two who were religious he talked about the bar mitzvah lessons, but there were others who took him for Christian. In the school yard one day, when he was in the eighth grade, just after he was bar-mitzvahed Dan talked proudly to a schoolmate about his blond hair and patted it fondly. He said it made him look like an Aryan, wasn't that so?

About most things that mattered in his life—his parents, relatives, school, religion, girls—Dan almost never talked. But about his dream of himself in uniform, on parade, in battle, he could not stop talking. He would cry with fury when the boys mocked him and called him General, but the next day he would be back again, talking about armies and battles and West Point. He saw himself so, and it was so that he wanted his friends to see him. Every time he showed them his soldier-drawings, every time he risked contempt and ridicule with his "West Point baloney," he seemed to be pleading with them to believe, so that he could believe more securely, too, that this was really Dan Burros.

At P.S. 121, nobody did believe Dan Burros, they knew him too well, the little fat kid who lived in the corner house, just another little mouthy kid with some screwball ideas.

At John Adams High School Dan Burros was a success

scholastically. His IQ on entry into high school was graded at 134 and in 1952 at 135, high enough to classify him as a "gifted child." His school records show term marks of 85, 90, 95 in almost every subject. He failed one course; not surprisingly, in view of his abrupt rejection of religion at that period, the course was Hebrew. And the failure was almost certainly deliberate, if unconscious. One classmate, Joshua Fierer (now a physician), remembers the John Adams Hebrew class vividly, for he was himself one of the top students in it. It was the first course ever offered in the subject at John Adams.

"It was a very relaxed class," Dr. Fierer said. "The teacher wanted to give good grades, to prove the value of the course in order to have it continued. For anyone to have done poorly, he really had to be not trying at all."

Dan sat sullenly through most of the first year, got a 70, protested to his classmates the second year that he couldn't get his mouth around the language, earned a 75 for classwork, and then went on to throw away the scholastic credit for the course by getting a 57 in the mandatory statewide Regents examination. He told everybody he couldn't stand Hebrew, that German was the language for him; in German he was a 90 student.

The scholastic record was "college caliber," in the school administrators' jargon—honors courses in mathematics and English, extra project work, electives in foreign conversation (German), honors classes in biology, membership in Arista, the scholastic honor society. He finished forty-eighth in a class of 451, with a four-year average of 87.07, high enough to win him enrollment in any one of the city's four tuition-free municipal colleges, the door to career and profession and attainment for scores of thousands of New York youngsters, and the goal for which boys from poor families like the Burroses study and strive during their four high-school years, and for which their parents pray.

Dan had worked hard for his scholastic standing, even taking courses in the summertime for extra credit. And then he threw it away, in a gesture of contempt for what he "came from." He never applied for admission to a college. After graduation he enlisted in the Army.

College was for the Jew boys, he told his friends later, the Jew boys who were trying to duck the draft. (Despite his father's military career, despite his Uncle Joe's militant profession and the fact that several of his uncles had served in the armed forces, Dan was convinced that his own relatives were mostly cowardly and that this was a "typical Jewish characteristic.") West Point? Well, he applied, got a Congressional appointment all right, but he couldn't make it because of his eyes, he said, so while the Jew boys were going to college, Dan Burros would enlist and make officer the hard way.

(There is no record of Dan Burros ever having applied for West Point—no record at the Military Academy, no record in the offices of his Congressmen or Senators. All his life Dan kept the secret of his failure or fear to move toward his life's dream; all his life he kept saying that he had applied and been turned down because of poor eyesight.)

The gesture of contempt had been in the making when Dan was crying aloud his desire for strength outside himself, but it took roots in attainments he achieved at John Adams, successes that meant more to him than the jottings on his scholastic record. He attained many things in those high school years—a uniform, power of office that could be melded and reinforced with power of brawn, an acknowledged reputation as "somebody different," somebody who stood out from the rest of the high school boys because of what he stood for, a political philosophy that made him feel tall and purposeful, and the successor to Rabbi Appleman in the chain of mentors he needed all his life. Most of all, Dan attained the fortress of hatred for others, those who had "made him" what he did not want to be, the fortress from which men fight to deny the enemy within by laying about at the shadows without.

At John Adams, there were new boys and new teachers who did not have memories of him as the moist, raging little boy on the corner who always wanted to be a soldier. He was taken seriously. He put on weight and he put on muscle, and he used them. He was on corridor patrol and he was on "dawn patrol"—a monitor who helped open the school. When students are unruly, monitors are supposed to report them for disciplinary measures. Dan developed his own style and he was remembered for it—he didn't report students, he "took care" of them himself—a twisted arm, a little roughing up. There were complaints to the teachers and he was taken off the patrols. But it didn't seem to matter much. For the first time in his life he was known with fear and all his life he would tell the stories of how he kept the kids in line at John Adams. There were a few schoolyard fights that are remembered by his friends. Later, Dan was to tell of others, particularly one story of how he took on a Jew boy in the classroom, hit him on the head with a chair, bloodied him good, how the teacher "ran for her life" from the classroom, how they carried the fight to the sidewalk, how a crowd gathered, how Dan got a Coke bottle and gave it to the Jew boy over the head, and how the Jew boy ran. Nobody but Dan remembered that fight and there is no record of the teacher's charge, which might have been noted in the Burros file at the school.

He developed a way of talking out of turn in class, getting up during a lesson and walking around. ("More irritating than aggressive," in the recollection of Harry Confoy, the Dean of Students. "He constantly wanted to call attention to himself. He wanted to make himself well known; a real pain to most of the women teachers.") The complaints would go to the Dean's Office and letters would go out to the parents calling them to school to talk over the behavior problem; Mrs. Burros would come, never Mr. Burros.

Dan still drew martial pictures in high school, but the knights had disappeared. The drawings now were of German helmets, German soldiers, German tanks.

He was drawing them in his freshman year and in his sophomore year. And in those two first years of high school he began the collection that he added to, pored over, fondled, treasured—the collection of German insignia, German war pictures, German signatures and Nazi documents, bits and pieces of German uniforms and decorations. In those two first years of high school, the collection was mostly devoted to German Army material rather than Nazi party souvenirs, but the collection had begun.

It was not until his third year, the junior year, that life took on a sharp focus for Dan and he achieved another goal —putting himself into sharp focus for those around him. It was in the third year that he began to talk openly about the power and virtue of the German Army, to pick fights about World War II, to stand out in class and in the schoolyard as the boy who was the hard guy politically among the liberals, even among boys who thought they were conservative, the boy who had read the books that showed what was wrong with America and could quote from them.

The focus took on clarity in debate in the classroom and in Arista, the honor society. Arista met in the John Adams music room to talk about scholarship, fellowship, leadership. Dan took the floor once and brought up Senator McCarthy's campaign to remove books he thought politically questionable from United States Information Service Libraries. A fine idea, Dan said, and he talked on about the importance of "weeding our libraries of evil literature, un-American books." Most of the boys in the society disagreed and there was a remembered atmosphere of shock.

As the third year went on, the shock became less and less because Dan was developing a reputation as the school's political tough. There was an American history class taught by a man known throughout the school for his classroom emphasis on the Communist menace. About once a week the class was devoted to a forum on public affairs and the topic one day was censorship, assigned by the teacher. Lloyd Contract was called on first and denounced the idea of "clearing out" USIS libraries. At one point in the debate, with most of the students attacking censorship and McCarthy, the teacher flew into a rage, banged the desk with his fist, and said, "You want to see censorship, I'll show you some," and ended the forum.

In the history class, Dan listened at first, then as the weeks went on began to speak more and more passionately about his agreement with the teacher, about the menace of Communism. One day the topic for discussion was "Should Red China be admitted into the United Nations." Most of the boys in the classroom were in favor of admission, but they got little chance to speak. The teacher gave the floor to Dan and to a boy who agreed with him and they held it, refusing to sit down. The other boys got angrier and angrier, jumping out of their chairs, shouting, but they never received permission to speak. Finally, in triumph, the teacher announced that it had all been a "demonstration" among himself, Dan, and the other boy to show how Communists took over a meeting. Dan laughed hugely.

The teacher says he has no recollection at all of Burros, but Dan was to talk glowingly of him and his "influence" all his life.

Dan's reputation as a rightist spread from Arista and the history classroom to where he could really hold forth—the schoolyard, the streets where he walked to and from school with his classmates. The schoolyard became a kind of personal forum for Dan and the walks were continuous debates, always on two themes.

The first theme was the danger to the United States from "weakness." Dan had quotations at his fingertips. He would spend many Saturdays in the library and then during the week quote from what he had read—from Nietzsche about strength, from Spengler about the weaknesses of Western society, from magazines and periodicals about how Americans had to prepare themselves, arm themselves, against a takeover by the Communists. Over and over, Dan made the same point. Americans were weak, they wouldn't fight against an internal menace, they let Communists "push them around," they had to push back and real hard. A "real American" had to know how to fight, had to have military training. Words like "foreigners" and "aliens" began to be used by Dan more and more.

He talked about *Under Cover,* the book by John Roy Carlson, published in 1943 about Nazi and fascist activities in the United States. The book was an attack on Nazis and fascists, but Dan said as far as he was concerned, it showed not the evils of Nazism or fascism but the "weaknesses" of the United States, the "burrowings of the Reds," the need to fight Communism.

Sometime in the third year of high school, Dan developed another theme—the "truth" about World War II. Dan's truth about World War II, which he argued and expounded and shouted, developed and grew as the year went on. It came to supplant Dan's talk about the Communist threat. It didn't matter who was right, he said at first, and it didn't matter who had won. The "truth" was that the Germans had the best armies and the best generals—particularly Rommel, whose picture by that time was hanging on Dan's wall.

Then he began to talk about total power tactics. Lloyd said one day that it seemed senseless to him to bomb cities since the military machine remained. Dan said no, bombing cities was a smart idea—"It terrorized the people so they could not produce the goods."

There were times when Dan argued quietly, but most of his friends remember him shouting and at times trembling with excitement. Often his friends would end the argument —because he was too passionate and wouldn't listen to counter-arguments or because he always seemed to have the "facts," and the quotes to throw at them.

The "truth" about World War II grew from the superiority of the Germany Army and its tactics, into support of the Third Reich. Dan was eliptical about that and seemed unwilling to say exactly what he meant, but dropped remarks about how "propaganda" had distorted the picture of the Third Reich, how it had "enemies," how someday the truth would be known and villains would be heroes.

To the best recollection of his friends, he never said anything anti-Semitic until he shouted "Jew bastard" at Lloyd Contract that day in the yard of P.S. 100. Lloyd never knew Dan was a Jew.

At home, the collection of German souvenirs had grown into a collection of Nazi souvenirs. One day, in the final half of the last year in high school, Dan told Clarence Anspake that he "knew" of a boy who kept all sorts of Nazi things in his home—guns, swastikas, pictures of Hitler, so on. Clarence had no idea that the boy was Dan—or that Dan might be testing him out—and mentioned the collection to some of his teachers. Nobody looked into it any further.

Dan talked of Germany and then the Nazis, and he never stopped talking about his career as a soldier. He had lost his fears of mockery, because now people knew him as a man to remember, and he made it quite clear that he saw himself as an eventual battlefield commander, at home as well as abroad.

On August 12, 1954, Dan enlisted in the National Guard. He was the only boy in his class to do so. Guardsmen drill once a week and from then until graduation, Dan showed up at school in uniform on drill days instead of going home after school to change. His buckle glistened, his boots were mirrors.

Dan made no pretense about his desire for the boys at school to see him in uniform. On St. Patrick's Day in 1955, Mrs. Anspake was sitting in a car outside John Adams, waiting for Clarence. Dan had been given the day off because he was to march with his guard unit in the parade. But he came running out of school in uniform, on the way to the parade.

"Where are you going, O'Burros?" Mrs. Anspake shouted out the window. He paused for a moment and said, "Off to the parade, but I wanted the school to see this."

Dan Burros was a good guardsman. In Company I, 165th Infantry Regiment, he was an enthusiast for the drills and he qualified as a marksman in May of 1955.

Toward the end of June, 1955, Clarence Anspake, Lloyd Contract, Ronald Moloff, and Dan Burros received their diplomas in a graduation ceremony at John Adams.

On August 28, 1955, the phone rang in the Anspake house. It was Dan, at Army recruiting headquarters.

"I'm at Whitehall Street," Dan told Clarence. "I'm enlisting for six years. I want to get into the paratroopers."

"Do you think it's such a good idea?" Clarence asked.

"If I can't do this, nothing else is worth living for," Dan said. "There would be nothing else left for me to do. If I fail at this, there's nothing else. I can't do anything else."

Burros received his discharge from the National Guard to enter the Army, was credited with one year and sixteen days of guard service. His guard record read "Recommended for further military service." His health was listed as good, his vision corrected with glasses. There was a notation that parental consent needed by minors was obtained and there was a notation that a psychiatric test was "not required."

During the next year, Clarence Anspake received about six letters from Dan. They were carefully descriptive letters about basic training first, then about the paratroops. Dan said he had made twenty-one jumps, including three night jumps, and that once he was blown over a barbed wire fence and injured slightly.

The letters came less frequently then, but in September, 1957, Dan Burros wrote to Clarence from Little Rock, Arkansas, where he and his outfit had gone to preserve law and order in a city that had become a battleground over school integration. President Eisenhower had authorized the enforcement of a Federal court order requiring that Negroes be admitted to the formerly all-white Central High School and, on September 24, Dan and the other soldiers of the 101st Airborne Division arrived in Little Rock under the overall command of Major General Edwin A. Walker. Dan wrote Clarence that for the first time this was not just training, but dangerous. "For the first time I really feel like a soldier."

Clarence's mother saw Dan on TV once from Little Rock.

Bayonet fixed, he was escorting a Negro girl into Little Rock's Central High School.

In mid-March, 1958, Dan suddenly returned to Richmond Hill, saw Clarence, and told him that although he had enlisted for six years, "after three years they give you a chance to reconsider your enlistment." He said his father was ill, he was needed to help around the house, and had decided to quit.

Chapter Four

By the time any soldier is discharged from the United States Army, he leaves behind him a thick file—the service jacket. Into it goes everything the Army knows about him and everything he has accomplished or failed to accomplish from the day of his oath to the day of his separation—assignments, promotions, medical records, scores, tests, commendations, comments, demerits, rewards, punishments, aptitudes, weaknesses.

The service jacket of Daniel Burros has all these reports, files, scraps of paper by which the Army judges a man while he is in uniform and traces his life when he is out of uniform. These records are confidential and all the Army will make public is a summation of a man's record. In the case of Daniel Burros the only statement the Army makes public reads as follows:

> Daniel Burros, who claimed prior service in the New York National Guard from 12 August 1954 to 28 August 1955 as an enlisted man, enlisted in the Regular Army 29 August 1955 in New York City, New York, and was sent to Fort Dix, New Jersey, and assigned to Company D, 364th Infantry Regiment. In November, 1955, he was sent to Fort Bragg, North Carolina, where he serviced with Companies C, A, and F, 187 Airborne Regimental Combat Team, to February, 1956. He was then transferred to Fort Campbell, Kentucky, with Company F, 187th Airborne Regimental

Combat Team; reassigned to Company L, 187th Airborne Regimental Combat Team in March, 1956; and to Company C, 327th Airborne Infantry Combat Group, redesignated Company C, 1st Airborne Battle Group, 327th Infantry, where he served to date of separation on 14 March 1958. His next of kin are shown as George and Estelle [sic] Burros, parents, 111–58 119th Street, South Ozone Park, New York.

ACTIVE SERVICE

He is credited with active service as an enlisted man from 29 August 1955 to 14 March 1958.

BY AUTHORITY OF THE SECRETARY OF THE ARMY:

J. C. Lambert
MAJOR GENERAL, U.S.A.
THE ADJUTANT GENERAL

When he entered the Army, Burros was the sharpest spit-and-polish soldier in his outfit. His uniform was knife-sharp and his boots glistened. He knew how to handle a gun, he knew how to salute, and he was full of military lore and military law.

He was face to face with his dream of power and he reached out toward it. He became one of the elite, a paratrooper. All the things he had longed for—strength and power and respect and command—were within his grasp. He knew all the stories about generals who had started as privates and climbed, through strength, to stars on their shoulders.

In the beginning, the first months, there was the sense of exhilaration that came from doing at last what he wanted to do, the camaraderie of shared physical exertion. Other new soldiers were homesick; Burros felt at home in the Army.

And then, somehow, it all fell apart and the Army became a sourness in the mouth, one more rejection. Quite suddenly, he was not a soldier on the way up, a born leader of men recognized as such but something of an oddball once again.

Instead of admiration, laughter. The salutes were just a little too snappy and to the soldiers in the company barracks he seemed to cross that uncrossable line between giving the officers their due and enjoying it too much. Once in a while, not too often because he was good with his fists, they called him Brownnose Burros.

The terrible discovery came that the uniform itself, the beloved empowering uniform, was not enough. Other men could scramble through the obstacle course better than he, other men could shoot straighter, fight harder, learn faster. And other men could strut and talk in a voice of command even though they had no rank—and nobody would laugh. When Burros swaggered or talked with a bark, he just broke people up.

The Army, for Burros, became a kind of reality he had never encountered before—the reality of a broken dream, the reality of failure. In school, people had laughed at first, but he had been a good student and he had made himself known. In the company barracks, despite the marksmanship and the paratrooper's badge, people not only laughed at him but dismissed him.

The sense of panic grew in Burros and he tried desperately to make himself known by advertising his enthusiasms. He felt that certainly in the Army, in the military atmosphere, there were men who would share his visions of the glory of the Reich, and he showed around some of his collection—the German pictures, the Nazi medals.

The only impression he made was on one sergeant. The sergeant carefully looked over his collection. Then he told Burros that if he didn't put that junk away he would put him before a board for a loyalty check. The word spread in the barracks and Brownnose Burros became Der Führer.

Later, Burros liked to say that he quit the Army because he couldn't stand what happened at Little Rock, couldn't stand the sight of white soldiers "protecting niggers," pointing bayonets at white girls, and that he decided to get out. The fact is, however, that Burros already had been put down as a misfit, already had made up his mind to get out. He called attention to himself by an obviously doomed attempt at suicide—cutting shallow gashes on his left wrist. When that did not work, he swallowed twenty aspirin—about enough to work up a good sweat—and left a suicide note:

> I have swallowed twenty aspirin tablets. I consider this a fatal dose.
>
> I am taking my life as I have nothing more to live for. I had hoped to see the revival of National Socialism. I see now our case is hopeless.
>
> We can easily deceive the decadent democracies, but the Soviets are the new Herrenvolk. Now that there is no more chance for the NSDAP [National Socialist Deutsche Arbeit Partei], I no longer have a motive for saving the forces of the decadent democracies. To them I will eternal damnation. I go to my Führer Hitler, Der Grosse in the Third Reich that endures forever. Sieg Heil. Heil Hitler.
>
> *Dan Burros.*

Looking back, some of the men who commanded Burros in those years have had to pay him the crushing, unwitting insult—they don't remember him, they don't remember his suicide attempts. They know he was under their command because the records say so, but he is just a forgotten name.

Burros' last commander, Major (then First Lieutenant) David S. Grossett, does have a recollection:

"He was a loner. He didn't fit in physically, mentally, or

socially. He just wasn't with the other men. He was never real aggressive and he wasn't in good physical shape, at least not for a paratrooper. Actually, his build was against him. He couldn't run well and he didn't have good coordination. His glasses made him look intellectual, which doesn't help when you're with two hundred aggressive young men. He didn't run to the towns with the other men when he had a pass, but I don't know what he did with his free time.

"He was in my office a few times for minor difficulties. I always felt he was listening but already had his mind made up about everything. I thought he felt somehow: 'You're giving the lecture, go ahead and talk. I have to stand here and listen, but I don't really have to take it in.' "

After he was discharged, Burros liked to tell his friends about how tough he had been. He loved the story about how a snake bit him and the medic said it was okay because he was obviously alive and how the lump on his foot got bigger and bigger. The punch line, of course, was that the snake died.

He told them he "put on" acting like a psycho by trying to strangle the company mascot, an eagle. "I tried to figure out some way to get out, so I grabbed the old eagle and I started choking the hell out of it, shaking it up and down and everybody was running out and said, 'He's choking our company mascot.' "

There was no strangling of the company mascot listed in Burros' record as the reason for separation. The story is told in a document in the service jacket dated January 2, 1958, from the office of the Chief of Neuropsychiatric Service, U.S. Army Hospital, Fort Campbell, Kentucky, and it reads:

> I certify that this is the report of neuropsychiatric examination in the case of SP-3 Daniel Burros, RA21964144, who was seen at this service. After careful evaluation, the diagnosis was found to be emotional instability reaction, chronic

severe as manifested by inability to deal with the minor stresses of normal duty, impulse suicide gestures, and poorly controlled anxiety and hostility. LD: No EPTS. [In Line of Duty: No etiology prior to service.]

This 20-year-old enlisted man was admitted to the Neuropsychiatric Service because of a suicide gesture. This is his third such attempt in recent months. The first time superficial cuts were inflicted by a razor blade, the second time overdose of aspirin, and the third time saw a return to the razor blade.

This man's early background perhaps predisposes him to great immaturity . . . as a result, this man has never learned to stand on his own feet. This man has gradually become increasingly unhappy with the service and longs for discharge. He admits quite frankly that he wants to get out and "will use any methods necessary, even if I have to kill myself."

Psychologically, this man is essentially an immature, emotional, unstable person who is engaged in much childish fantasy. He tends toward impulsive actions and is obviously unable to handle stress in a mature manner. I do believe that he is pretending to be more disturbed than he is. However, it is unlikely that punishment or counseling would help this condition. The immaturity is of such severity and such chronicity that his retention in service will only result in further failure to adjust. He should be separated from the service at the earliest date. It should be noted that in spite of his seemingly peculiar behavior he is not psychotic and is not truly suicidal. In my opinion, the soldier is not insane, possesses sufficient mental capacity to know the difference between right and wrong, should be able to adhere to the right and refrain from the wrong and is considered to be mentally responsible for his acts. This condition is not amenable to hospitalization, treatment, disciplinary action, training, transfer to another station or organization or reclassification to another type of duty. This soldier has no mental or physical disease or defect which warrants disposition through medical channels.

Recommendation: It is recommended that no further attempt at rehabilitation of this soldier be made since it is believed that he is useless to the service and further such attempts would be of no avail. This soldier should be placed before a board of officers with a view to separation from the service under the provisions of Art. 635–209 because of unsuitability.

Captain Carl B. Schleifer,
Medical Corps, Psychiatrist.

From the recommendation of the board of officers meeting to consider the psychiatric officer's report on SP-3 Daniel Burros' suicide attempts:

The respondent does not possess the required degree of adaptability for military service. . . . he is unsuitable for further military service career.

Discharge: Under honorable conditions by reasons of unsuitability, character, and behavior disorder.

Clarence Anspake saw Burros a few times after he returned from the Army to Queens. Dan had put on weight and looked puffy and sloppy. When the two young men played chess, Burros did not try hard and would give the game away. He did not seem to care about his clothes or the shine on his shoes.

Chapter Five

Dan's friends—those who remembered him from school days and the new friends he made later in the strange world he entered—were to say that he had been "influenced." Influenced by militarism, influenced by a teacher, by books, by the Army, by extremist magazines, by Nazi literature. It seems closer to the truth that the books and the teaching and the philosophy of might were what he had been seeking and seized, when found, to give a structure and meaning to his own needs. They were influences, but only in the sense that the pieces of wood and branch that a castaway on an island weaves into a protective hut are influences against the cold and the night.

Four years from the day of Ezekiel to the day of "Jew bastard" and another four years to the board of officers meeting in Fort Campbell. Eight years of running. But the flight had not begun at the Congregation Talmud Torah, any more than it ended in the schoolyard of P.S. 100, or in an Army camp in Kentucky. It began with a death, a trial, and an imprisonment—the death of Jesus Christ, the trial of His tribe, the imprisonment over two millenia of the Jew within the mind of the Jew-hater.

The bits and pieces of the kaleidoscope of Dan Burros fell into a pattern identifiable by psychiatrists long before the report written by the Army doctor—the frustrations that built and simmered to the point where he could only express them with his fists, the compulsions to expose the weaknesses of his desires for military leadership to the inevitable mockery of his friends, the pendulum of rage and joy, the rejection of self and the search for strength outside himself, the passionate identification with those who would destroy him, the eternal need for symbols that would cloak him and protect him. They were classic symptoms of a neurotic personality, the personality of self-directed hatred.

The study of the neurotic personality has one major importance and significance—what it tells about the normal personality, the thread leading backward through the maze of the mind to the daylight. The neurotic personality is the normal personality blown up under a magnifying glass.

The fact of being Jewish is an environmental ingredient in the development of personality, a herb thrown into the stew that can either be overpowered by other ingredients and in the end merely a kind of memory or scent, or be of such strength that it comes to dominate the taste and aroma of the dish. In the case of Daniel Burros, Jewishness was the most powerful ingredient because his entire life was to be dominated by it.

Jewishness is—a race, a religion, a people, a philosophy, a heritage, a parental descent, an outlook. The arguments among Jews never end, each Jew seeking an answer that will either identify him with Jewishness or allow him to slide away from it a bit, as his needs dictate. But every Jew will say that whatever else it is, Jewishness is an experience. In some it is an experience around which life revolves, in others —fewer—an experience blended into a variety of experiences, and in some an experience raised to the shock level of trauma, occasionally or day in and day out. There is a kind of universal, broad denominator, quality of Jewishness that all Jews share and there are national Jewish experiences of enormous importance but based on the chance of where a man happens to be lucky enough or cursed enough to be born.

Dan Burros had been in flight eight years at least in identifiable time when the board of officers met—and the Jewish ingredient in his personality was long fixed. The separating out, dissection, of the Jewish ingredient in one neurotic personality tells something, perhaps, of the experience of Jewishness itself, the thread leading back through the maze.

The American Jew is different from the French Jew and the French Jew is different from the Moroccan Jew and the American Jew of eastern European parentage has a background that turns him into a somewhat different individual from the American Jew whose parents came from Germany or England. These differences are not so much of national character as of the way their forebears were treated nationally, and the memories and lore and fears or securities they passed on to their children.

Money affects Jews quite as much as it affects Gentiles—more, since it often is the one haven, instead of a series of inherited battlements surrounding the personality. Money affects Jews and makes those with it rather different from those without it—money and status and profession and the family island.

But there are experiences and sensations and reactions that are common to virtually all Jews—American, German, Moroccan, shoemaker or banker—and that are woven into the Jewish condition. The fact that there is a Jewish condition disturbs many Jews and they rail against it, but it is a fact nonetheless, because it cannot be otherwise. It is a condition not inborn but created, created not so much by Jews but by Gentiles, and arising from the one simple fact that, being apart, Jews have no privacy. Take a piece of paper and put an indelible dot upon it; the paper was "born" blank, but the dot remains in its fiber, even if it is inked over or bleached with eradicator.

Of these experiences and sensations, one of the most important is the very fact that creates the basis of the Jewish condition—the fact that the Jew is not considered exactly the same.

The non-Jew reacts and speaks and thinks of the Jew as two things—a human being liked or disliked, and a Jew. If that is not always so, the Jew has enough sensation of it having been so in the past to think often it is so at the moment, so the result is quite the same.

In the Bohack's supermarket in Richmond Hill, when a mother calls "Richard" or "John" to her child, there is no thought connection set up simply as the result of the name. If she calls "Irving" or "Isaac," she is saying "Jewish child" and everybody within the sound of her voice has an instant connection—Jewish child. Something additional has been added to the child, a quality beyond mere existence as a human, and something additional has been added to the awareness of others, Jew and non-Jew, to the child and mother. The something additional need not be antagonism, but it is a differentiation and the unending sensation of differentiation is an ink dot on the paper.

Jean-Paul Sartre wrote in *Anti-Semite and Jew:* "If a Jew is fascinated by Christians it is not because of their virtue, which he values little, but because they represent anonymity, humanity without race."

Men seek distinctiveness, but they seek a distinctiveness they have created themselves to answer their talents or desires or ambitions, not the distinctiveness of the mark on the forehead. There are Jews who have so sublimated their Jewishness, have such fear of it or so little need of it, that they are scarcely aware of it. But they recognize the mark of the Jew in other Jews and that reminds them of themselves as something additional, as human and Jewish, and so they are deprived by what is outside of the inside privacy and for that instant are not just human beings but Jewish human beings. What is a Jew? A man with no solitude in himself.

"Even in America," the old Jews used to say when something went wrong, or was not to their understanding or expectation. Even in America, the Jew is bereft of the sweet boon of privacy and carries, or feels he carries, the mark of differentness. Sometimes the mark is a hidden thing, a scar. Every Jew who has ever been kept out of a hotel, or heard of a Jew being kept out of a hotel, or heard an anti-Semitic remark in the streets or a club, or read of one or sensed the momentary pause on being introduced—a pause that might have come from interest or sympathy, or simply awareness and not distaste—is conscious of his separateness. It is a separateness created, not earned, and he detests it; above all he wants to be simply one with the humanity around him, but he cannot achieve it. His name or his face or the names and faces of other Jews—he knows that these create automatic distinction in the minds of Jews and non-Jews, and he cannot escape entirely from the chill of automatic separateness to the family warmth of automatic acceptance.

"Even in America" there are daily, and quite proper, national reminders of separateness. He is an American and a Jew, but the life of the nation often is in a rhythm where non-Jewishness is the essential beat. Christmas and Easter are part of the beat, and he is a listener, not a dancer. The most solemn occasions involving the symbol of statehood—the Presidency—are centered on non-Jewishness—the funeral of the slain President, the President at worship. The histories and great traditions of other nations, their foundations, are entirely outside the realm of Jewish experience—what does a Celt mean to a Scottish Jew, or Saint Joan of Arc to a French Jew, or coronation in a cathedral to the English Jew? In America, newness sets him apart too—"land where our fathers died," children sing in school and when the Jewish child is old enough he asks wistfully—*our* fathers?

Solitude is an absolute and like most absolutes cannot ever be entirely achieved; only the catatonic is entirely alone. The non-Jew in America never achieves entire inner privacy, but he is born with enough of it so that he does not suffer from its total attainment. The Jew does—but in America, even the Jew has enough formal and social recognition as an individual in himself, through law, tradition, and a national belief in egalitarianism and kindliness (a belief is not practice necessarily, but a belief, existing, is a reality), so that the pain of unwanted distinctiveness varies sharply, like a fever curve. Sometimes the pain is so acute that he longs to hide his face. But in America, in many men and at many times, the pain diminishes almost to the point of absence. The Jew in America cannot be entirely private, but he can be defiant or amused, and most of all he is a proprietor of the most important manifestations of a society—its laws.

But no number of laws, no strength of others' traditions, and no faith in morals or even religion, can protect the Jew —German Jew, Russian Jew, Brazilian Jew, and American Jew—from knowing that he was born into a tribe of victims. His own religion can give him faith in the infallibility of Jehovah and he can take whatever comfort he can from the conviction that somehow the gas chamber was a reflection of God's will and God's power. His strength can give him determination that he will not allow it to happen to him. But, from the moment he is aware of his Jewishness and of the history of Jews he is aware that that history is the biography of the scapegoat, the martyr, the dispossessed, the wanderer, the outcast, the tortured, the despised or the pitied, the beaten, the murdered—the victim.

What is a Jew? "A misfortune!" There is not a Jew who has not said that to himself, sometimes in a whisper he can hardly hear—and if he sometimes denies that it is true of himself, he cannot but know that it has been true of others. Every Jew now alive has lived in the memory of the ghetto's stench, remembers Torquemada, and every Jew now alive has an Auschwitz number on his soul. Worse, every Jew now alive has known himself unable to save his wife and mother and daughter and son and father from the ghetto, from the fire and the slave's tattoo—and if by chance they still live he looks at them and fear and self-contempt eat at him because he fears that if the madness comes again he will not be able to fulfill himself as a man by saving them.

What is a Jew? "A disaster!" This is part of the bitter humor, which is truth's tear, of Jews in every land. The Tunisian Jew Albert Memmi writes in *Portrait of a Jew:* "The Jews of Algeria say with a bitter smile: 'Racism is like the trolley from Saint-Eugene: it runs through the whole town, the beautiful sections and the ugly ones, it goes very fast . . . but it always leads to the cemetery.' "

The Jews have told mocking stories of what it is to be a Jew in every country and every time. In New York: The old Jew sits in the subway and a Negro sits down and pulls out a copy of the Yiddish newspaper, the *Forward.* The Jew stares as his black neighbor reads and finally, unable to contain his curiosity, nudges him and says, "Pardon me but I can't help asking—are you by any chance Jewish?" The Negro stares coldly at him and answers, "What's the matter, I haven't got enough trouble?"

What is a Jew? A Jew, among other things, is a prisoner caged in the ugliest of cages, the mind of his own enemy. The enemy is the anti-Semite and over and over Jews ask, "What is an anti-Semite and why is he?" They struggle for the answer because there is almost nothing more important in their lives to understand, but most often they cannot comprehend, any more than the guppy in the tank comprehends the approaching piranha—the guppy sees the piranha, knows him, knows the fate approaching, the teeth, but comprehension of the killer born is beyond the comprehension of the victim born, the victim the killer so desperately needs.

The first step in comprehension is to examine the nature of anti-Semitism. It is founded in need. Religious need, political need, national need—the need of institutions that betrayed their own weakness by their very dependence on a crutch, in this case the Jew.

The greatest irony in all of recorded or mythological history is that anti-Semitism began in the death of a being, whether God or man or the Son of Man or the Son of God, who was good, who was of the covenant, and who was a Jew, on the cross of Jesus. It was not the act of crucifixion that created anti-Semitism but the deep longing, which grew into a religion, to understand what the crucifixion meant.

Jesus died to save men's souls—not the souls just of Jews but of all men. His death is not simply the foundation of Christianity, but its act of creation and essence. His death was beyond martyrdom, which implies mere passivity, but philosophically and theologically an act of volition and of necessity. He died to show the way and if he had not chosen to die, if God had not decided to sacrifice His Son, the way could not have been shown.

All who believe in Christ, his Passion and Redemption, owe their salvation to His death and, therefore, to His crucifiers—and since Christianity so believes, to the Jews. All mankind shared the guilt, it is taught, but the Christian mitigates his guilt by belief in the meaning of the sacrifice and the Redemption. He mitigates it, but he deepens it, too, because of all men in the world, only the believing Christian benefits by the death of Christ, because only he is guided by that death to salvation.

The Jew, for Christianity, is the reminder of the shared guilt, but he is more guilty than the Christian and his presence on earth is needed—as a reminder, as an assurance that the degrees of guilt are relative. Throughout medieval history, the Popes who preached that the Jews must suffer for their sins and obstinacy also insisted that they must survive as example, and gave them ghetto refuge.

The Jew, to the believing Christian, is *of* Jesus, of His time, His tribe, and His suffering. Judaism is the acknowledged father of Christianity and, Freud believed, the vehicle for father-hatred. But he is a father who can be hated in safety and security: is he not a father who deserted his children?

Religiously, the Jew became the marginal man—important to the society but condemned to live on its physical and emotional outskirts, much the same as the untouchable is the essential marginal man in India. The caste system rejects the untouchable for the sins he has committed in earlier incarnations, but he is the very basis of its pyramid. Caste without untouchability is a contradiction in terms, like slavery without slaves, the pagan without the sacrifice, Christianity without the Jew.

Men may debate the religious need for the Jew; it is difficult to deny Western civilization's political need for him and that this need was part of the essence of anti-Semitism. Politically, the Jew was not only a convenient scapegoat but something more—a focal point for national identity. There is no "in" without an "out," no club without the blackballed. The function of the Jew in medieval Europe, in Czarist Russia, in Hitler's Reich, was to be placed by the ruler outside the club of nationalism so that all others might value and understand their membership.

There is indeed a certain logic to the selection of the Jew as the enemy of nationalistic leaders. In every country there were Jews who wanted to become part of the nationalistic fervor of the country, but inevitably they were rejected because the nature of Jewishness made the Jew more logical as enemy than participant. Nationalism depends on three things—difference, militarism, proprietorship.

The Jew as the wanderer and the dispossessed longed for proprietorship but could not achieve it except on paper, and paper is made to be torn. The Italian Jew could buy a piece of land and that sliver belonged to him. But it never belonged to him in the sense that land belonged to the Italian peasant whose fathers and sons had been born on it and experienced ownership not in the feel of papers between his fingers but rising up from the earth. The French Jew may feel he owns a piece of property. The "Frenchman" feels he owns the entire country, and this is beyond purchase. It is important to make sure that the Jew cannot truly own a part of the nation because if the wanderer can claim proprietorship then in what way is the man of generations born better?

Nationalism emphasizes, by its nature, the differences among nations, races, clubs. It is based on emotionalism and the glorification of irrationality.

The Jew desires acceptance as a human being, his salvation lies in the universality of humanity. He cannot allow himself the luxury of irrationality because it leads away from universality toward divergence and schisms. Nationalism is doctrinaire and authoritarian, universality is liberal and permissive.

Nationalism depends on militarism, not simply for conquest but for the discipline it needs, out of the lack of other strength, to bind the nation together. In Jewish biblical history there were Jewish conquerors and armies and imperialism. But the religious life of the Jews centers on a paradox—the torment of the Chosen People. The enemies of the Jews achieved victory and power, the Jews suffered defeat and the destruction of the Temple and dispersion. If armies were important, and conquest, the suffering of Judaism was not only in vain but a symbol of God's rejection.

It was unthinkable to question God's justice, lest the edifice of Judaism, based on Jehovah's omnipotence and infallibility, collapse. It was unthinkable to consider the rejection of the Jews by God, since that, too, would be beyond conception—God's destruction of His own covenant. The answer for the Jews had to be that somehow in His wisdom God had found them lacking and though he would not, could not, reject them, He was testing them in the fire of persecution to make them worthy of His love. The persecutions have no meaning except as instruments of the mystery of God's punishment. Conquering armies are as pebbles in God's hands, to be scooped up and thrown into the sea at His desire. Truth is power and truth lies in the acceptance of God's will and the study of His word—the rationale for what is seen by Jews as piety, by nationalists as meekness, by psychiatrists as masochism.

Just as there is no crime without the criminal, there is no anti-Semitism without the anti-Semite. There is no one anti-Semite as there is no one Jew. Men have acted against Jews through fear or ignorance or lust or greed or to demonstrate to themselves that they belonged, for all the reasons men are driven—or drive themselves—to crime.

Hatred or fear of the Jew has been so much a part of the history and breath of life of Western civilization that it has become almost a part of the human environmental condition. It exists, most sadly perhaps, among people who are not aware of its existence within them. The psychiatrist Rudolph M. Loewenstein writes in *Christians and Jews:* "At some point in the course of analytic treatment almost all non-Jewish patients will manifest varying degrees of anti-Semitism."

What concerns the Jew most about anti-Semitism—it is often said by men of goodwill that anti-Semitism is a Christian problem essentially; it did not seem so in Auschwitz—is what goes into the makeup of the conscious anti-Semite. It is the mind of the conscious anti-Semite that organizes and catalyzes, that transforms the abstracts of historical, religious, or national conditioning into the reality of the pogrom and the gas chamber.

The circumstantial evidence is that anti-Semitism is a mental disorder, because the anti-Semite sees certain human beings not as human beings but as objects. They are reflections of his own needs and passions and his inability to recognize them for what they are is such a severe form of irrationalism as to be a symptom of mental malfunction. The anti-Semite suffers from a fear of demons, but since he is not aware of his fear is convinced of the reality of demons—a clinical example of paranoia.

That is the psychiatric explanation of conscious anti-Semitism, skeletonized. Sartre has provided a kind of character sketch of the conscious and eager anti-Semite and although it may not be clinically demonstrable in every aspect it has the virtue of being immediately recognizable:

He is a man who is afraid. Not of the Jews, to be sure, but of himself, of his own consciousness, of his liberty, of his instincts, of his responsibilities, of solitariness, of change, of society and of the world—of everything except the Jews. He is a coward who does not want to admit his cowardice to himself; a murderer who represses and censures his tendency to murder without being able to hold it back, yet who dares to kill only in effigy or protected by the anonymity of the mob; a malcontent who dares not revolt from fear of the consequences of his rebellion. In espousing anti-Semitism, he does not simply adopt an opinion, he chooses himself as a person. He chooses the permanence and impenetrability of stone, the total irresponsibility of the warrior who obeys his leaders—and he has no leader. He chooses to acquire nothing, to deserve nothing; he assumes that everything is given him as his birthright—and he is not noble. He chooses finally a Good that is fixed once and for all, beyond question, out of reach; he dares not examine it for fear of being led to challenge it and having to seek it in another form. The Jew only serves him as a pretext; elsewhere his counterpart will make use of the Negro or the man of yellow skin. The existence of the Jew merely permits the anti-Semite to stifle his anxieties at their inception by persuading himself that his place is marked out in advance, that it awaits him, and that tradition gives him the right to occupy it. Anti-Semitism in short is fear of the human condition. The anti-Semite is a man who wishes to be pitiless stone, a furious torrent, a devastating thunderbolt—anything except a man.

The criminal is a man who lives outside the law and society and has at least the strength to do so. The anti-Semite is a man who wishes to commit criminal acts and seeks a license to do so. The license is anti-Semitism. He accuses the Jew of murder in order to be allowed to murder him, of cowardice in order to kill his children, of greed to rob him, of betrayal to betray him. Anti-Semitism is the image of the anti-Semite.

What is a Jew? A man on trial. The great triumph of the anti-Semite is that he is the criminal who has succeeded in accusing the victim of his crime, of placing him on trial for that crime, of having the victim accepted as a evildoer—and, perhaps most hideous of all, of making the victim wonder whether, after all, he is indeed what the criminal says him to be.

Any man accused, be he innocent or guilty, is on trial and the Jew is an accused man. Christianity accuses him either of the death of Christ or of willful refusal to acknowledge the suffering and sacrifice of God, which is an accusation of the betrayal of the father by the son.

Most Jews eliminate that from their own burden of guilt and for Christ and Christianity feel fear rather than sorrow or responsibility. They cannot dismiss from their consciousness the realization that through the ages others have regarded them as deicides.

But that is just the historical beginning of the accusations against the Jew on trial. He is accused of cosmopolitanism and tribalism, of miserliness and of ostentation, of cowardice and of bullying, of not belonging and of pushiness, of being thick-skinned and of being whiningly oversensitive, of capitalism and Bolshevism, of not getting his hands dirty and of working too hard, of being blind to truth and of being just too smart, of stealth and of boasting, of unmanly passivity and of complaining martyrdom—whatever unpleasantnesses exist in the human condition have at one time or another been portrayed as Jewish characteristics, and usually all of them together.

No, none of this is true, the Jew cries, or if any of it is true it is because I am a man not a Jew and it is no truer of me than of any other man. He cries, No, no. He knows it is false because he has but to look at the faces of his children and know that they are children as all other children.

But to greater or lesser degree—the triumph of the anti-Semite who passes some of his corruption to the healthy—the accusation creeps into his soul. It cannot be otherwise. For two millenia, the accusations against the Jew have filled the air he breathes. He reads books in school, where anti-Semitism has the authenticity of casualness and the authority of the classics—Shylock and Fagin. He knows that the churches have taught Christ killed by Jews, he has seen the long-nosed cartoons, he has seen the pictures of the mounds of the dead and he is ashamed they died without fighting. The literature of the West has the thread of accusation running through it and so does its religion and so does its history. Men of valor and wisdom, heroes in their national history were anti-Semites and repeated the accusations. Decades, centuries, millenia of accusation and trial and punishment produce guilt in the victim.

Albert Memmi wrote in *Portrait of a Jew:*

> Confronted with myself, I was by no means sure of my complete innocence. There is a certain independence between the clear motives of an accusation and the feeling of being accused; between the reality of the offense and the blame one takes for it. The blame has vagueness, the formlessness and the unfairness of a nebulous halo effect. Let us not forget in passing that if I want to rid myself of this whole question I shall not only have to confound my accuser but I shall also have to dissipate the fog in other men—and in myself. The result, in any event, is that constant ambiguous feeling that scarcely ever leaves me no matter where I am: I am both of this world and not of it; I long passionately to be of it and I never hope to be completely. Better still, I distrust that integration. With this opinion of me how far will groups or masses, small circle or nation, tolerate my participation. The very question, the very anxiety, rob me of my

spontaneity, prevent me from living naturally as others do. To be a Jew is also that: to be a Jew is to be set apart from other men, it is also to be set apart from oneself.

After Christ, the history of the Jew is in large part the history of anti-Semitism. In this history, there are occasional footnotes—recordings of Jews who became anti-Semites. Jews have paid little attention to these Jewish anti-Semites—"What's the matter, I haven't got enough troubles?"

But there have been occasional psychiatric examinations of anti-Semitic Jews and of these one of the most revealing was written in 1946 by the Norwegian-born psychiatrist Dr. David Abrahamsen. In *The Mind and Death of a Genius,* Dr. Abrahamsen examines the life, work, and character of Otto Weininger, a Viennese intellectual whose essays and psychological studies made him briefly famous and who shot himself in 1903, in the house where Beethoven was born. He was a Jew, he was an anti-Semite, and he was twenty-three years old when he died.

Otto Weininger was an assimilated Jew. His father thought of himself as a Jew, but his children remember his anti-Semitism. Otto became a convert to Christianity and his anti-Semitism became part of his writing. Dr. Abrahamsen ties Otto Weininger's Jewish anti-Semitism to Weininger's confusion over the most fundamental relationship, that between man and woman. Weininger was a homosexual and like most homosexuals sought desperately to denigrate women. Dr. Abrahamsen wrote of Weininger's psychology-philosophy:

> Weininger now arrives at the culminating formulation of his problems, namely the question of the importance of being a man or a woman. His answer is that the relation between man and woman is that of subject to object. Woman seeks her consummation as the object. She is the plaything of husband

and child and is anxious to be no more than such a chattel. Furthermore, this contrast between subject and object in the theory of knowledge corresponds ontologically, Weininger believes, to the contrast between form and matter. He considers woman significant as the material on which man acts. She is matter, is nothing, and her importance lies in meaning nothing. The abstract male is the image of God, the absolute something. The female (and the feminine element in the male) is the symbol of nothing. Such is woman's place in the universe.

He adopts a like concept of the Jewish people. He believed that even the most superior woman is immeasurably beneath the most degraded man. This pattern is repeated in his contention that Judaism at its best is immeasurably beneath even degraded Christianity. In Judaism he sees a spiritual movement, a psychic constitution, and he tries to prove its existence by anti-Semitic arguments. He says that everyone who has thought over the problem of woman and the problem of the Jew must be astonished to discover the extent to which Judaism is penetrated by femininity. As the soul is lacking in woman so is it lacking in the Jew. For this reason, Zionism is without hope. The Jew, like the woman, has no ego. Both lack greatness. Both live in the family and not as individuals. In them sexuality is always present; woman and Jew are concerned with mating. They also seek to make other humans feel guilt. Ours is not only the most Jewish but also the most feminine of all eras. Modernity of the spirit is Jewish from whatever viewpoint it is considered. Weininger asserts that ours is the most anarchistic of all times; there is no sense of state or of right; history has no meaning. The struggle in the future will be between Judaism and Christianity, between business and culture, between form and personality. These are the two poles. There is no third alternative.

Dr. Abrahamsen also writes:

In the final analysis the contempt and rage of Weininger were directed against himself. He felt weak and powerless,

> filled with anxiety. He had constantly within him the fear of impotence and a feeling that he was castrated (castration complex.) In general this feeling of castration is the deepest unconscious root of anti-Semitism and it was the basis of Weininger's monstrous anti-Semitism. His wild hatred of women also rose from the same feeling . . . Weininger sought passionately to deny Judaism because that would mean to deny self. Basically the denial of his mother religion was also directed against his mother, whom he hated.

From all of this, the nature of anti-Semitism as seen by historian, theologian, philosopher, or psychiatrist, Dan Burros cannot be separated. Nor can he be identified neatly and exactly with any one case history or sudden insight because he had his own pattern, his own torment, and his own needs.

All his life, Dan Burros was in desperate, haunted search of the one goal no man can ever truly reach—exterior strength, power outside the self.

The record of his short life shows that never since his childhood did he believe himself strong enough, worthy enough, to survive as himself. As himself, he was not simply defenseless, he could not make himself known. To make others aware of himself, he had to reach out and hit them, thus crying, "Here I am, see me, feel me."

But that too failed him—the fights in the streets and in the schoolyard because he was small and tubby and not terribly frightening, and people laughed. He searched for something else that would project him as an individual—"See me as victor, see me as something better, different, this will prove my existence." The chess games were so important that sweat broke out on his forehead, but victory could not help him make others see him so he could see himself because his victories were so small and the others really did not care.

It came early to Dan Burros that there was a way to make himself known, and thus to know himself as existing. It came to him that there were men to whom other men granted fear and respect—men of arms. There are exterior symbols and instruments of strength immediately recognizable as betokening manliness, strength, belonging—weapons, uniforms, posture, and bearing.

The man he admired most, his father, was a proud, wounded veteran and the desire for emulation certainly was part of the need. But George Burros was a man who enlisted to fight a known enemy at a time of war. His son Dan had no enemy except within himself, no war except against himself.

Dan Burros saw the armor external to himself clearly and reached out for it. He drew pictures of men in uniform and men in battle—and whatever the face on the drawing paper, it was Dan Burros who marched in uniform and who gave battle and who was, therefore, to be feared and known.

The need was so great and the weakness so great that the symbols of strength and, thus, of fulfillment became fetishistic in his life. The fetishes were the pictures of generals and tanks, the boxes full of medals and bits of uniform. Dan Burros was not an overt homosexual, but it was within him to collect and cherish exactly and only the photographs and bits of metal and cloth that glorified masculinity and masculine potency. When he was in the National Guard, drilling one day a week, he could have gone home to change, but he came to school in uniform—came to school dressed as a man.

But every man who wears a demonic mask knows the frightened human face beneath. Dan knew his own face. He drew pictures of himself as warrior but saw the reality of himself, as walking hand in hand with his mother to and from school. He dreamed of himself as victor and saw the reality of himself as the comical kid on the block. He talked of himself as the West Point cadet and saw the reality of himself as so fearful that he never really would make a serious effort to get into West Point, because he saw his failure ahead.

Dan Burros searched for the explanation of what was "wrong" with him, why he could not be big and strong and powerful and feared and known—and discovered it.

It was ready-made for him, in the fears of persecution that his grandparents carried with them to the New World, in the very fact of their flight from their homeland. It was ready-made for him by the miasma of fear in which all Jews have lived since Hitler. It was ready-made for him by the tradition of obedience to law and God's will taught to him at the Talmud Torah of Richmond Hill. It was ready-made for him in the history of Jewish permissive universality.

Everything that was "Jewish" in him was weakness to him and blocked his way to the power he needed and sought. Is not a man who is persecuted and must flee, who is the perpetual victim, who bows in humility to God's rod, who lives in fear of his contemporaries, who seeks so nervously to convince all about him that all are equal, who is pacific and shoulders arms with a sigh, is not this man a weakling? And if that is the man within Dan Burros, how can Dan Burros, seeking strength, feel anything but hatred for him?

Most men hate something of what is within them, but most men do not find the world telling them over and over, "You are right to hate yourself." Dan Burros did. A Jew, he was on trial. As a man of weakness, he sought explanation for his inadequacies. He found the explanation of his weakness in his Jewishness, and convicted himself—of existing as he was. He despised the weakness of the victim and the one overwhelming irony of the life of Dan Burros was that he became an example of the quintessential Jewish victim—the Jew who confesses that the diseased fantasy in the mind of the anti-Semite is truth.

Having confessed, Dan Burros sought to escape punishment. The only way he could do this was to identify himself with the aggressor, the man of strength, and become himself a judge of the Jews. To survive as he wished to survive, he had to destroy his enemy and his enemy was the Jew. The enemy of my enemy is my friend. The enemy of the Jew was, historically, the nationalist and the militarist, and Dan Burros identified himself with them. And, within his own lifetime and within the daily consciousness of all living Jews, there was an enemy far more frightening—far more potent—than anything in history, and that was Nazism.

The Nazis were the accusors, judges, torturers, and executioners of the Jews. Thirsting for the torment and execution of the Jew in himself, Dan Burros fled to them. They would help him kill the Jews and they would give him the greatest gift, the death of a particular Jew.

Chapter Six

In the Queens Borough Public Library on Parsons Boulevard—about three miles from where Dan Burros lived with his parents—there was a small lunchroom where employes ate the sandwiches they brought from home. Burros used to bring his in a tin lunchbox, and every noon would take out a thermos of coffee and a sandwich. It was always the same sandwich, tuna fish, and it became a little joke among the people in the catalog department, who usually would lunch together—Dan and his inevitable tuna fish.

"If I ever brought anything else I would have to make up my mind every day what to bring," Burros would tell people who asked him why always the same sandwich. "This way, I bring tuna every day and I don't have to make up my mind." It was a small instance of Burros' craving for regimentation, even if it had to be self-imposed.

Burros' colleagues thought it rather eccentric, but they were getting used to his odd behavior. Burros had started to work in the library on July 10, 1958—four months after his Army discharge. He was an operator of office equipment machines. He had picked up the printing trade during the spring of 1958—possibly, for some obscure reason of his own, studying under an assumed name; the Manhattan School of Printing, the private institution where he claimed to have studied, had no record of Daniel Burros.

Burros' job was to print catalog cards. He earned $3,680 a year and he had a reputation as a good worker. He arrived promptly at the library every morning at eight thirty and rarely missed a day's work because of illness. He also had a reputation, which he cherished and fostered, as a Nazi.

When he finished his sandwich, Dan would spend the rest of his lunch hour sketching. It was always the same picture—a Nazi soldier in complete gear, helmet, gun, knapsack, and swastikas as decoration. Over and over, the same picture. The only time he ever drew anything else was at Christmas time, when he drew a background for the office Christmas tree on a large sheet of blue paper—three kings, trees, snow. Everybody said what a good job, everybody liked it.

Dan liked to talk, but always about the same subject—Nazis, Jews, race, Germany. As it happened, there were no Jews among his colleagues in the department and no one attempted to silence him, so Dan would go on and on about how he hated the Jews, how Hitler was absolutely right. He would talk about his hatred for the Jews during coffee break, whenever there was a free moment, and at lunch. There were no Jews in the department, but there were two Negroes. When they left the table, he would look after them and say, "And the Negroes are next."

He would giggle a lot when he talked about how the Jews would get it, but he never laughed when he talked about his collection. On Saturdays he would roam New York's junk shops and antique stores looking for souvenirs, and one Monday morning he came in to work with the announcement that for five dollars he had purchased "Hitler's party badge." He said he had his collection hidden away in boxes in closets and that his mother, if she ever found them, would throw them away. He and his mother did not see eye to eye, he said, although she was a German; she would throw out certain "pamphlets" that came for him in the mail, and he had to rent a post office box. His mother, he said, argued with him all the time about his ideas.

The dream was to go to Germany and one day he said happily that he had seen an advertisement for a trip to Germany for just fifty dollars. He went down to the tourist office and came back dejected; the fifty dollars was only the down payment.

Sometimes the other members in the catalog department would try to argue with him or reason with him and this he loved. He would rush up to the reference room and come back with armloads of books to prove his points—the worthlessness of religion, the treachery of the Jews, the Reich's greatness.

In January of 1960, after he had worked at the library for about a year and a half, Dan suddenly turned on a superior who had given him some instructions about catalog cards, said he would not do it that way, and walked out of the library. He never came back. A few weeks later, somebody called from the North German Lloyd Lines, saying Dan Burros had applied there for a job. The caller's curiosity had been aroused because Dan, when asked to demonstrate his drawing skill, had sketched a Nazi soldier. Dan didn't get the job. He then applied for a job as a multigraph operator with the U.S. Navigation Company, the shipping agent for the North German Lloyd Lines. He worked there from January to May of 1960. He started at seventy dollars a week and was later raised to seventy-five dollars.

By the time he left the library and started working for the shipping company, Dan's reputation as a Nazi had spread—to the New York City police.

The New York police have a special branch that keeps a careful eye on extremist groups in the city. There is a particularly high danger potential from extremists in New York because it is the home of the United Nations and a stop on the itinerary of almost every foreign dignitary visiting the United States; it is the duty of the New York police to try to make sure that the United Nations delegates and the visitors are not annoyed.

The special branch takes extremists with complete seriousness. The detectives who work for it believe that most of the fringe members are bigmouths, but they believe, too, that these men and boys live in an atmosphere in which terror is so often discussed as an instrument of "policy" that it takes on reality. The talk of guns and dynamite and sniping and "getting the enemy" becomes ever more a part of the environment of some of the extremist groups—ever more a part of the preventive actions by the police. The branch watches for symptoms—crank letter writers, people who buy many books on guerilla warfare. There is a whole subworld of racists who correspond with each other, trade racist magazines and advertise in them. Wearily, the police say that sooner or later all the "nuts" come to New York for the publicity.

In December, 1958, five months after he was employed by the Queens Borough Public Library, the name of Daniel Burros entered the files of the special branch. He was sending out letters on stationery marked Post Office Box 121, South Ozone Park. He signed them with a round rubber stamp: "American National Socialist Party," and a swastika. The party consisted of Dan Burros and it was a kind of a uniform for him. He got in touch with other one-man parties around the country, became known among members of the Nazi fringe, who spend a good deal of their time simply writing each other letters.

From fringe periodicals and from letters he got the names of German officers and Nazis around the world. In his billfold, stuffed with Nazi mementos, he carried a small autographed picture of a man called Colonel Hans Ulrich Rudel, and a photographic reproduction of a note Rudel sent from Cairo to Burros. It simply thanked Burros for his letter, told him he would be happy to visit him if he ever journeyed to the United States. Many of Burros' letters were from former German paratroopers and one such came from a Colonel Bohmler, who thought Burros could assist him in getting a manuscript published. Burros obediently complied with Colonel Bohmler's request, offering the manuscript in a polite letter to Bennett Cerf, of Random House, whom Burros may or may not have been aware was a Jew.

Dear Mr. Cerf:

I am writing to you on behalf of an acquaintance of mine —a German Colonel (retired). He wishes to have his book published in America. It is entitled *Monte Cassino* and is naturally about the battle of Monte Cassino in the Second World War. The author commanded a German parachute regiment in the battle. The book has already been published in Germany by E. S. Mittler & Sohn, Frankfurt/Main and a motion picture was made from the book in Germany.

I feel this book has great possibilities of success in America. The book would certainly be of interest to the many Americans who served in the Italian Theater of Operations. I think at this time many people would be interested in reading the German side or version of the battle, especially when written by a parachute officer. This book would also be of interest to many Roman Catholics because it concerns a Catholic Monastery.

I have no experience in the line of representing authors and I am only representing Colonel Bohmler as a favor to an officer I admire. He asked me to put out feelers to American publishers. I wrote first to you, because I liked your personality on television and I thought you might be the one to handle this.

If your firm is interested I will bring over a copy of the book (as published in Germany of course) and the rest of the negotiations can be carried out with the firm of Mittler & Sohn, etc. in Germany. If Random House does not handle this sort of translation perhaps you can recommend another publisher. I send a stamped, self-addressed envelope for your reply.

Thank you very much for your time.

Sincerely yours,
Dan Burros

An equally polite note from a representative of Mr. Cerf promptly went back to Burros, explaining that a book had recently been published on the same subject, and declining Colonel Bohmler's manuscript.

Another German paratrooper with whom Burros got in touch was a man called Josef H. Maguiera, who had been dropped into Poland in the early hours of World War II. In January of 1959, Burros received a letter from Maguiera, saying he would be visiting the United States and would like to talk to Burros about reactivating the German-American Bund. They met in a park late at night. Burros told him he was interested and Maguiera—who said he was working in Germany as a butler—admired some of the Nazi pictures Burros had with him. Later, Burros wrote to Maguiera, but the correspondence apparently lapsed.

In addition to his letters, Burros subscribed to a number of British fascist papers, German rightist periodicals, and in early 1960 he joined his first fascist party. From the British National Party he received card No. 564.

To some of his correspondents, Burros wrote not only about his hatred for the Jews but about his contempt for Christianity. The idea of a "Nordic religion" based on the "pure" gods of war and force cropped up in some of his letters. Among the fringe fascists in the United States there are a number who "specialize" in Nordic mythology and symbols. Burros wrote to one of them, a woman, dating his letter German fashion "29 Marz 1960":

> I thank you so much for your letter. I agree with you that Christianity was a great disaster for the Nordic. This doctrine is alien to him and destructive to his nature. I myself am a bitter enemy of this doctrine of weakness—for that is what it is.
>
> I would like very much if you could sometime give me what your husband thinks a good program for a Nordic party would be. I would like his detailed political views. I have very great respect for his views and I think I could learn a great deal from him. I have of course my own ideas, but I am still young and still can learn a lot. Only a fool is not anxious to learn. I admire Hitler very much, but one of his faults was he wasn't willing to listen to others.

Dan had begun using an alias in some of his letters—Hans Friedrich Borchers. He picked the name from John Roy Carlson's *Under Cover,* still one of his treasured books. Carlson had listed Hans Borchers as one of the Nazi agents operating here in the thirties, during the boom period for espionage.

The New York police were fascinated readers of some of Burros' hate literature. Every now and then Burros would get letters from anti-Nazis, people who were frightened and furious at the proliferation of the hate groups and who acted as private undercover agents. They would write to men like Burros, posing as Nazis or anti-Semites and pass their letters on to the police, along with the replies—in Burros' case almost always denunciations of the Jews.

Occasionally he would send contributions of a few dollars to fringe groups. Once he sent some money to John Kasper, an acknowledged racist who had opened a bookshop in Washington where he handled anti-Semitic publications. Burros' letter was too enthusiastically pro-Nazi even for Kasper, and he returned the money, saying he didn't want to have anything to do with Nazis.

By that time Burros had for several weeks been living two lives, in two cities. New York was the city where he earned his living, but it was a shadow to the real substance of his life, in Washington, D.C. To the people he worked with he was a queer boy with ugly ideas who drew strange pictures. To the police, he was a part of the crackpot file, a fanatic who wrote letters to other fanatics. To his mother and father, he was a heaviness, the good boy to whom something terrible was happening, a sickness of some kind they feared to examine too closely but which they prayed would pass. He didn't talk much to them, and when he did it was talk they didn't want to hear. He was their son, their only son, sick or healthy. It would pass, it would pass.

But Dan Burros knew what he really was. He was a storm trooper, Storm Trooper Dan Burros, official disciple of Adolf Hitler, soldier, apostle, and valued aide to the man who would carry on the betrayed dreams of Der Führer.

Early in 1960, Burros began making regular weekend trips to a frame house in Arlington, Virginia, that was to become his place of employment, his shrine, his home, his platform, his nest—the headquarters of the American Nazi Party. He scrapped any ideas he had about forming a New York Nazi party and became part of the tiny group—sometimes six, sometimes a dozen—of young men who lived a barracks existence in the Arlington house, part of the atmosphere of quick crushes and quick feuds, uniforms and symbols and pledges and forays into Washington for street brawls and publicity.

For months he was a kind of novitiate, earning the right to take the vows by participating in picketing with anti-Semitic signs—the White House was a favorite target because of its publicity value. He got the Nazi equivalent of battle stars—four arrests and ten-dollar and twenty-dollar fines for disorderly conduct, and one real medal, a one-hundred-dollar fine and a suspended sentence of six months for defacing the property of the Anti-Defamation League with swastika stickers.

In June of 1960, less than a month after leaving his job at the U.S. Navigation Company, Burros combined his two lives into one; he left New York City to live in Arlington.

The four hundred dollars he had in his wallet when he left New York went quickly, but in September Burros found a job in Washington, as a multilith operator with the Chamber of Commerce of the United States. He listed three Nazi friends as references, wrote "public speaking" under the heading "Additional Qualifications and Experience," and under languages wrote: *"Ich kann Deutsch lesen, und auch kann ich ein bischen sprechen!"* He passed the intelligence and proficiency tests with high marks and two days after he filled out the application was put to work at a salary of seventy-five dollars.

Burros then filled out his formal application for membership in the American Nazi Party. He wrote that he had been given psychiatric observation by the United States Army "because of my national socialist beliefs" and was found mentally competent but unfit for military service. Under organizations, he listed the Airborne Association of Fort Bragg, the British National Party, and the "Hilfrufgemeinschaft, Enemaliger, Waffen SS Germany," an organization to help veterans of Hitler's SS troops. The organization was his own invention.

He listed his father's first name accurately as George and gave his mother's name as "Erika Renate Schroder." He defined his reasons for joining: "I wish to preserve the white race and combat the forces of Jewish bolshevism which seek to destroy our race and nation." He was accepted into the party and took the "Trooper's Oath":

> In the presence of the Great Spirit of the Universe and my Loyal Party Comrades, I hereby IRREVOCABLY pledge:
>
> TO ADOLF HITLER, the philosophical leader of the White Man's fight for an idealistic and scientific world order against the atheistical and materialistic forces of Marxism and racial suicide, *I pledge my reverence and respect.*
>
> TO THE COMMANDER of Adolf Hitler's National Socialist Movement, *I pledge my faith, my courage and my willing obedience.*
>
> TO MY PARTY COMRADES, throughout the world, *I pledge my absolute loyalty, even unto death.*
>
> TO MYSELF, as a leader of the White Man's fight, *I pledge a clean and manly life of honor.*
>
> TO THE UNITED STATES OF AMERICA, *I pledge my loyalty and my careful compliance with its Constitution and laws* until those which are unjust can be legally changed by winning the hearts of the people.
>
> TO MY IGNORANT FELLOW WHITE MEN, who will hate and persecute me because they have been so cruelly brainwashed, *I pledge my patience and my love.*

TO THE TRAITORS TO MY RACE AND NATION, *I pledge swift and ruthless justice.*

The oath was administered by the "commander," George Lincoln Rockwell.

Chapter Seven

There was a little money in the barracks of the American Nazi Party one summer Saturday in 1960 and George Lincoln Rockwell, founder and self-styled commander of the party, decided to take some of his boys to get something to eat at Mario's Pizza Parlor a few blocks away from the headquarters at 928 North Randolph Street in Arlington.

Rockwell ordered a sandwich and turned to another counter to get a pizza. The counterman told him to get out.

"You mean you refuse to wait on me?" Rockwell demanded.

"Mr. Levine has ordered no one to serve Mr. Rockwell anymore."

Rockwell grinned delightedly and turned to Burros, John Patler, and a couple of the other troopers with him.

"Well, boys," he said happily, "I guess we will stage a sit-in."

All the way back to headquarters, Rockwell was full of exultation.

"Those stupid Jews. Those stupid, stupid Jews. I've been looking for something like this for weeks and now they've handed it to me on a silver platter."

They stopped at a shopping center where Rockwell invested some of the unspent pizza money in white cardboard. Back at headquarters, he scribbled the slogans for placards and made his ritual telephone call to the police to announce his plans, while Patler and Burros lettered the signs and thumbtacked them to sticks. Rockwell ran about urging everybody to hurry. Then everybody put on swastika armbands, piled into Patler's car, and rushed back to Mario's to do battle.

Up and down in front of the pizza parlor Rockwell, Burros, and Patler marched with their signs: "What's the matter, Mario, won't you serve people who expose Red spies?"

About twenty people gathered to heckle the troopers. Mario's went to the attack: a man began hosing down the sidewalk—and any trooper who happened to be marching by. Rockwell, not quite goose-stepping over to the enemy's combat position, found himself drenched.

Furiously Rockwell rushed to a policeman standing by. The cop looked him up and down slowly and said that Mario's had a perfect right to clean its sidewalk and, anyway, he wasn't about to let a "public nuisance" like Rockwell tell him his business. The crowd loved that and Rockwell turned red with anger. The damp troopers kept marching, watching their commander for orders. After an hour, retreat was sounded.

At headquarters, reviewing the action, it was obvious that the main objective had not been obtained—publicity. But Rockwell, suddenly struck by an idea, announced a tangential victory for the cause: "At least we cut down on Mario's business for an hour." And one trooper, a man called Roger Foss, said that "two or three people passing by on the bus smiled at us." Then everybody agreed that it had been, all in all, a pretty good little action.

Life at the barracks centered on incidents like the Battle of the Pizza Parlor. It was an atmosphere in which reality and fantasy and wish-fulfillment merged until nobody could quite tell them apart, nor wished to. The boys would sit around talking about how one day they would run the whole damned country. In the meantime they played with their toys—"training": reveille and uniform inspection and decoration awards, the cleaning of the guns, standing guard. But it had to have a purpose and the purpose was the little forays into Arlington or Washington—picketing the White House, speeches on the Mall in front of the Washington Monument denouncing Jews, putting up swastika stickers here and there, doing battle with places like Mario's.

Then the most delicious part, getting together again at headquarters and "reviewing the action." Boy, I socked that kike good in the nose, did you see the blood? We'll get lots of publicity out of this one, did you see the reporters and the photographers? Man, this is real! Next time, we'll really show them!

Once in a while, somebody would say, ah, hell, it didn't amount to much, and the others would glare at him. He had interrupted the play, but for a moment only, until they could push what he had said out of their minds and once again warm themselves in the rich fantasy.

The man who had created the atmosphere in which this fantasy could be nourished was—and is—a symbol and a symptom of his time.

George Lincoln Rockwell is a symptom of two political phenomena, one of them universal and as timelessly a part of the human condition as illness, the other indigenous to the United States and as symbolic of the mid-twentieth century in America as TV commercials.

Universally, Rockwell is merely a minor representative of the ageless impulse of men and women eaten by the disease of hatred to find a political expression or rationalization for their malady, that particular malady that sees other human beings as objects of gratification or opposition to oneself rather than as separate human beings.

They have existed in every age and in every country, people who are drawn to politics not primarily for purposes of administration or even of power but for outlet of the hatred-pressures building up within them. These pressures create a number of distinct and important needs—the need to search out others who see life the same way so that they can feel they are not alone and not abnormal, the need for acting out their aggressions, and the need above all for what they can take as a tangible structure and understandable rationalization for the turmoil within them. To explain their own feelings of guilt, on which hatreds are always based, they need a definable enemy who can shoulder the responsibility for them. It is not very dissimilar from the sexual pervert attracted to small girls, who convinces himself that all the little girls of the world are full of evil and deliberately set out to tempt men, so that molesting them becomes not the gratification of an obsession, a thought he cannot live with, but a justifiable act of retribution and punishment.

The man who is obsessed with hatred is a far more fortunate individual than the sex-obsessed pervert. History has not glorified the child-molester, but history has raised statues to emotional perverts—the dictators and inquisitors. The child molester must keep his illness secret, but there are in most countries, including the United States, no laws against expression of the hatreds of the emotionally ill and no laws against their acting out their aggressions against others, so long as they do not resort to physical violence. This last point is indeed a frustration because it prevents the haters from reaching their emotional climax in violence. The frustration is to some degree compensated by the fact that there are so many of the haters that they can easily make contact with each other and so enjoy a kind of group paroxysm.

Part of the search for structure and rationalization, obviously, is the quest for others so afflicted who are gifted with powers of dramatization, verbalization, and explanation of aggressions, and who can create the arena for acting them out. These men become the leaders of the hate groups and for their followers supply important services, providing outlets and avenues of gratification and above all, assuring them that what the rest of the world may take as illness and weakness is, in fact, health and virility.

Rockwell is of no particular distinction or special interest. There are scores of "leaders" like him in the United States and most of them have larger followings, more organizational ability, better public arousement talents. There is, however, a certain clinical political significance in Rockwell and his American Nazi Party in relation to American society. It lies in the fact that he and his small band are forced to rely almost entirely on the highly developed and specialized techniques of advertising, press agentry, and mass communications, as well as on the degree to which he has been able to use them. The extent to which the Rockwell group exists at all in the consciousness of the American public depends completely on these techniques. It is not so much a movement as a skywriting—when the plane is aloft and trailing smoke the slogan can be seen. It vanishes soon in currents of air and then ceases to have visible physical existence. The slogan does continue to exist for a time in the minds of the people below, but unless the plane goes aloft or the commercial is repeated through other advertising devices, the slogan fades from the mind as it does from the sky.

The utter reliance of the Rockwell group on publicity grows out of its position in the American political tradition—

or rather, its lack of position. The political manifestations of the hate-illness in other countries were able to take on substance and power because they could present themselves as expressions or heirs to important specific conditions in their countries—upheaval following defeat in a war, economic collapse, revolution, xenophobia, religious persecution, class warfare, fear of invasion.

In these countries, the specific conditions created deep divisions within the society, or uncontrollable fears. In the sociological jargon, these in turn led to "polarization"—the splitting of the society into immediately identifiable groups with opposing interests. Distrust and hatred are by-products of the emotionally disturbed. In many countries, over the centuries, there was almost no period in which these suspicions did not exist and, therefore, over the centuries the politics of the sick did not merely find an acceptable environment but became in truth a built-in part of the environment.

This meant that the leaders of the haters were able to develop programs tailored to the needs and desires of an important segment of the society, essential to the attainment of power. They could offer programs that were built on conquest, or militarization, or dominance by one of the polarized segments, or satisfaction of resentments of one group against another. In the process, they could also offer plunder to the group with which they were identified, plunder of the rest of society. In brief, there was a real mutuality between a torn and frightened nation and leaders who spoke and breathed division and fear.

The conditions that made for identity of interest between the leaders of the sick and the rest of the nation do not exist as immediately and specifically in the United States. It is not that there are no divisions within American society. Quite the opposite. There are so many varieties of national background that each depends for its individual existence on the existence of the others, and taken together they add up to an entity different from all its parts. A coral reef is made up of millions of separate creatures, each of which retains its separateness but helps create a oneness. Militant nationalists always preach that the danger lies in "mongrelization," the security in homogeneity. Exactly the reverse is true. Steel without alloy is brittle. The strength of the United States has been in its very mixture, which has prevented a clear break.

The mixture in the nationalities of the United States has led to other patterns of mixture, which protect it against the danger of polarization. There are two major parties, but each has its liberals, conservatives, and reactionaries. Men and women in American society for the most part do not carry the brand of their class in the way they talk and the way they dress, the education they receive and the entertainments they cherish.

There are two groups outside, two groups that do not blend into the mixture and enjoy its savor—the poor white and the Negro. But the difference between the United States and the countries where hatred grew into a way of political life is important here, too. In other countries, the emphasis was on keeping "out groups" out. In the United States there is recognition that maintaining the barriers preventing economic progress of the very poor whites and complete social admission of the Negroes weakens the country. The Negro revolution is not a revolution of total upheaval. It is a revolution only of timing and pace, because its goals have been recognized and accepted by those chosen to govern the country.

Any mixture can be spilled or spoiled, any society broken.

It is simply that in the United States the fact of mixture has prevented the Rockwells from being able to find any group fearful enough and yet powerful enough to identify with. They have been unable, therefore, to develop any program that has any concrete meaning or that promises any important satisfaction to any important group. The Rockwells are outside the candy store in the United States, their noses pressed to the window.

Lacking a program—the desire to attain power is not in itself a program—Rockwell and people like him must resort to constant skywriting. They must attract attention or vanish, and attention itself becomes not only nourishment but the goal.

Over and over, Rockwell has told his band that they must get in the papers, must get radio and TV coverage, must get magazine attention. The nature of the exposure does not count—they must be seen and recognized and heard. Every article in every newspaper, including those denouncing them, is cherished and chortled over because it is evidence of their own existence.

The craving for publicity is more than an obsession, it is a necessity for survival, like water for a thirsting man. It has become the pivot around which the band turns and has shaped all its activities. It has, among other things, put the Rockwell group into a strange kind of parasitic relationship with liberal and left-wing organizations.

Without a detailed program of his own, Rockwell must feed, for publicity, off the programs and activities of his enemies, the liberals and the radicals. Eagerly, Rockwell and his lieutenants search the papers for activities they can picket. Picketing is the major form of their enterprise, because it is safely within the law, but to get attention they must picket where the talents or the programs of the liberals and the left have focused attention and thus draw some of the spotlight on themselves.

Where a controversial play or movie is opening, the Nazis rush with their signs and uniforms—to the Boston opening of the movie "Exodus" or to the New York opening of the play "The Deputy." The controversy and the high-level audience usually guarantee some press attention, which spills over onto the Nazi pickets. The objective, of course, is to foment some kind of ruckus that will lead to a minor riot and more pictures and press attention.

Rockwell has written a 440-page autobiographical testimonial to himself. Both in his autobiography and to psychiatrists who examined him in the summer of 1960 (the result of a court order), Rockwell was candid about his background and beliefs. Unlike Daniel Burros, whose career as a Nazi was a masquerade and much of whose energy was, therefore, necessarily bent on concealment, Rockwell glories in self-revelation.

Rockwell was born in Bloomington, Illinois in 1918, the oldest child of "Doc" Rockwell, a successful vaudeville comedian. Rockwell regarded his father (so he told the psychiatrists) as "a great guy" who intellectually understood him, was intelligent, likable, humorous, vibrant, and healthy—and, in his vaudeville act, joked about the Jews. Rockwell's mother was Claire Schade, a toe dancer, who was divorced from her husband when Rockwell was six years old. He described his mother as feminine, small, weak, and easily bullied, but claimed to have had a good relationship with her, never to have exchanged a harsh word with her, and to have felt protective toward her; nevertheless, he never quite forgave her for making him wear short pants when other boys his age were in knickers. He had a brother two years younger, with whom he fought jealously, and a sister four years younger with whom he got along well.

As a boy, Rockwell traveled around the country with his parents. He attended Hebron Academy in Hebron, Maine, and spent about three years in Brown University, before enlisting in the Navy. He became a pilot, serving in the South Atlantic and Pacific. After the war, he was a sign painter, cartoonist, salesman, organizer of a magazine for servicemen's wives, and did other jobs, none with conspicuous success. He was married twice, divorced twice.

During the Korean War he was recalled to service. (After he became a Nazi, a Navy board discharged him from the Reserves.) During this tour, the pro-Nazi ideas that had been fermenting in his mind took shape. From that point on, his life revolved around making contacts with pro-Nazi Americans. Unlike Burros, who was interested in any Nazi contact—mainly through correspondence—Rockwell looked for Nazis with money, who could sponsor and support his activities financially. He had a variety of sponsors, falling out with almost all of them.

His own estimate of his intelligence, like Burros', was quite high. In his autobiography he wrote:

> A truly superior mind, which can apprehend the mightiest facts and ideas in the universe—facts which are unthinkable to the millions and billions of human beings, can surely perceive its own relationship to those depressing billions of empty heads. Such a great mind can surely realize its own attitude with regard to the wormlike minds which squirm and crawl by the billions in the mud of life. And when such a mind becomes thoroughly aware of the gift which Nature has bestowed on it, it is an act of gross dishonor to make a mealy-mouthed pretense to be "just one of the stupid herd" in order to curry favor with the army of idiots and be able to lower one's eyes "modestly" while the forces of organized

> boobery extoll one's genius. . . . In exactly that sense then I am prepared to set forth my story, the good with the bad. I am neither afraid to admit my mistakes nor am I afraid to lay claim to my own genius. What the world may be not yet ready to admit, I will wring from it by simple demonstration, in combat.

By the time Burros went to Washington to make the party his life in early 1960, Rockwell had found a sponsor to put up the money for the house on North Randolph Street. He had moved his headquarters around a great deal—his own house, apartments he shared with followers, almost always in Arlington. Arlington was just right for Rockwell—geographically almost a part of the capital, where the publicity was, but a little less expensive, and, Rockwell believed, in the more amenable climate of Virginia.

North Randolph Street met one important specification—it was zoned for both residential and commercial purposes. That meant that Rockwell and his troopers could live there and also use it as the site for their only important piece of equipment—their printing press.

It was a ramshackle white clapboard house, two stories and an attic, with a small gray front porch, and an empty lot in the back where the boys could march around. In front of the house, the troopers put up two steel flagpoles, one on either side of the porch, from which they flew two Nazi flags. In back of the house was a little shed where the troopers held bayonet practice.

On the ground floor, there was a wood-paneled front office with Nazi banners and photos of Hitler and several rooms where troopers flopped. There were a couple of desks, one of them used by J. V. Kenneth Morgan, Rockwell's deputy.

The Commander lived on the second floor—in a room that had an iron frame bed with half the slats broken, a spindly table, a typewriter. On the floor there was usually a pile of dirty clothes and two or three black leather jackets, papers, and mail. Some of the troopers lived in another bedroom upstairs, sleeping on mattresses on the floor. In a third upstairs room there was a long table and stacks of literature.

The house had been purchased by Floyd Fleming, a Washingtonian, for $21,500 and the seller was Rose K. Hall, a real estate broker with a reputation as a right-wing sympathizer. The monthly payments were two hundred dollars.

The main purpose of the headquarters was to serve as a printing center for Rockwell. It was here that the American Nazi Party printed its stationery with the swastika letterhead, its leaflets denouncing Jews, and some segregationist broadsides: ("White man! Are you going to be run out of your nation's capital . . . without a fight?") The little *National Socialist Bulletin,* consisting mostly of pictures and accounts of the exploits of troopers, and the manual for the storm troopers, was printed at a Washington shop.

Burros was quickly accepted into the fraternity; there was no doubt at all about his fervid passion for Nazism and he was an "A-Number-one" Jew-hater. He was eagerly willing to devote all his spare time and most of his money to the cause —and Rockwell had found that most of the visitors who came to tell him how great he was, how much they were willing to fight for the Nazi movement, did nothing more than talk. The few who would work and live with him were his corps, his jewels, and until they left he treasured them all.

For Rockwell, Burros had a particular importance—his training as a printer and operator of office machinery. Sometimes Rockwell would tell some of the boys that maybe Burros was a little too fanatical and too touchy but let him alone, he was valuable for his trade and training, and was working on "The Book" by the Commander.

Everything revolved around Rockwell—the work, the forays. The passions and the hatred revolved around him, too, and the little band of troopers fought to get his ear, to set him against the others, or to get a promotion or a decoration or a word of praise from him. They often grumbled about him—about his drinking, about how he took the best food for himself, about how he was so moody, up and down, up and down—but he was the pivot and the master for the men, who needed both in their lives.

At headquarters there was a constant formation, splitting, and regrouping of cliques, and the troopers spent a considerable amount of their time gossiping about each other and telling tales to the Commander.

Most of the troopers were, like Burros, in their early twenties, and several of them were married. But in their ideas, attitudes, and conversation their most pronounced common characteristic seemed to be a kind of suspended adolescence.

Burros' closest friend at the headquarters was a man his own age, a New Yorker named John Patler—born Patsoulis—who joined the Nazi band when he was in the Marine Corps. Patler, a slim man with a head like a skull, dark features, taut as a wire, fancied a streak of romanticism in himself; he named one of his sons Horst Wessel, after the German Nazi godling. For a time he managed to combine his Nazism with his role as a husband, but when his wife, who kept house for him near the barracks, sickened of the Nazi movement, Patler, like many others of the Rockwell band, eventually chose the barracks over marriage.

Patler didn't think much of Burros in the beginning. Burros looked sloppy much of the time and liked to lie around with his trooper boots on the furniture. One day Rockwell wanted to take a group photograph and Burros dressed up in the party uniform, on which he pinned some German World War II patches. Patler didn't like the idea of wearing non-issue on the uniform, complained to the Commander, and refused to pose for the picture.

Patler was a printer by trade and that drew him to Burros. He was also quick with his fists, which Burros admired deeply. One day Patler got into a fist fight with another trooper, Seth Ryan, behind the barracks and Patler's undershirt was bloodied. Burros was ecstatic about the fight and begged Patler for his undershirt, which he put away and treasured. (Patler later said that Burros had egged him on to fight Ryan by telling him Ryan was saying things behind his back. Patler said Burros detested Ryan and "he just was crazy about getting that undershirt with Seth Ryan's blood on it." After the fight, there was a "hearing" about it called by the Commander in front of headquarters. "All the time," says Patler, "Dan Burros was on the porch pacing back and forth with his right hand in his pocket and I later discovered that he was carrying a loaded pistol in his pocket. He told me later that he was very afraid that they would all try and gang up on me or him, and he said if they did, he was going to pull out that gun and start shooting. He said he'd kill them all and he had this loaded gun he was carrying in his pocket.")

Another man with whom Burros feuded was James Conrad Warner, who was about twenty-five years old in 1960, a flabby, fuzzy-cheeked boy with close-cropped hair, who later split with Rockwell and wrote a long pamphlet denouncing him. Warner didn't change his anti-Semitic or pro-Nazi ideas, he just didn't think Rockwell was moving toward power the right way and his pamphlet was full of denunciations of Rockwell, whom he called the leader of the "smear-bund," and of whom he said: he "looks like a mongrel of some kind . . . thick nigger lips."

There was a fight between Warner and Burros one day, but from all accounts not much damage was done by the two tough troopers. They circled around each other, feinting, until the other Nazis, including Rockwell, who were looking on, got bored.

In his pamphlet, Warner got his own back at most of his former comrades. Burros, whom he identified by a code letter V, was called "a weirdie trooper whose life ambition is to put Jews and niggers into the Gas Chambers, although he looks like a Jew himself and would never give his home address for the party files. He runs around the house cutting pictures out of magazines and newspapers and gets his kicks out of choking the party dog."

The dog, a mongrel called Gas Chamber, was the subject of some controversy at the headquarters of the American Nazi Party. Burros and others complained that Rockwell was feeding the best food to the dog while the troopers had to live mostly on Corn Flakes and water. (Food was a topic second only to *Der Tag;* whenever he had any money Burros would gobble a bagful of hamburgers or go off by himself to eat a couple of steaks.)

The troopers, including Burros, also thought that Rockwell was eating too well, but it was easier to take it out on the dog. Burros used to say that it might be a good idea to cook Gas Chamber. "That dog looks better all the time," Burros would say. "We have to do something. That dog eats better than us. What the heck, we can take him out and chop his head off and have him for supper."

Some of the troopers would laugh, but there were some literal-minded humanitarians in the group who were horrified. They would listen to Burros talk about plans for killing all Jews in gas chambers. Burros was named "extermination" planner and loved to draw pseudo-scientific pictures of gas chambers and tables of organization and timing for the executions. They listened to Burros talk about his dream of a torture machine consisting of a piano whose wires were connected to the nerves of Jews; the Jews would twitch and jump to the tune of the piano player. That was a pretty funny one, they thought, although sometimes they told him not to talk so much in front of the uninitiated. And they would examine the little green-wrapped bar of soap Burros carried in his pocket. It was marked in German, "Made from the finest Jewish fat." But when Burros threatened to cook the dog, they all agreed he was going too far.

Patler and Burros had common fraternal cause in their dislike of Warner. Warner was editor of the party bulletin and Patler thought he could do the job a lot better. Burros' picture was supposed to appear in one issue, but Warner forgot to pick it up at headquarters and he telephoned Burros from the commerical printing plant where the bulletin was published to tell him that it wouldn't get in.

Burros was furious to the point of tears. He rushed up to see Rockwell and told the Commander that he was going to "knock Warner on his ass." Burros stormed around the house, kicking furniture and stamping his feet. Rockwell finally called the printer, told him to hold up until the picture could be sent over.

In addition to Burros, Patler, and Warner, there were a number of other regulars, some of whom lived in the barracks, others who spent their free time there.

There was Richard Braun, a tall, gangling man of about twenty-three who never seemed able to stop talking in a thin whiney voice about street fighting. "If you don't get a bloody nose or a black eye," he would say, "it proves you weren't fighting hard enough. . . . When I get a guy in a fight, you know I don't look like much, but I'm plenty tough, see . . . when I fight a guy I don't fight to kill him, you know, you know." He would stop as if his thoughts had run away, his green eyes staring, then poke his listener and start again: "You know what I mean, don't you? I'm going to mangle him. When I'm through he's just a mess, that's all. No good for nothing."

Roger Foss joined about the time Burros did, a thin wry man with sunken eyes and pinched features who said he came from Minnesota and claimed boxing talent—"I only need three punches. Two hit the man and the third hits the air." He loved to tell the story about the time he was working in a hotel in Fort Lauderdale, Florida, and one night shut the door in the face of a group of "big-nosed Jews." "Sorry, Jews, we are closed," he would say and chortle.

Foss regarded himself as an expert on Negroes, having taken notes on their street activities from the window of his room in Harlem. Foss had tried a variety of fringe groups before joining Rockwell but to his frustration had found they would not jump with eagerness at some of his suggestions for violence.

In deep despair, he decided that since nobody was fighting the Communists as he wanted to fight them he might as well look into joining the Communists. According to his own story he contacted the Soviets in New York and Washington and met one Valentin M. Ivanov, first secretary of the embassy, a "real good guy." The Russians apparently were not terribly desirous of Foss' allegiance, and he got in touch with Rockwell's group. He and Rockwell visited the Department of Justice and Foss registered as an agent of a foreign power. Rockwell obviously saw the whole strange episode as a good way of getting publicity and gave a whoop of delight when the first story about Foss appeared on TV.

"Christ, Commander," said Patler joyously, "do you realize the international significance of this?"

"You're damn right I do," Rockwell shot back. "Why, I'll bet there's a report on the American Nazi Party lying on Khrushchev's desk right now!"

Later, when Foss complained that Rockwell had passed up an opportunity to picket an address by Roy Wilkins of the National Association for the Advancement of Colored People—such a missed chance to get publicity for the Nazis—Rockwell consoled him. "Forget it," he said, "you've given us more publicity than a hundred pickets."

One of Rockwell's staunchest troopers was J. V. Kenneth Morgan, a heavyset man, who, in his mid-thirties was considerably older than most of the others. J. V., as he liked to be called, was a truck driver and a long-time member of a variety of fringe groups. Probably because J. V. enjoyed the distinction of being Rockwell's deputy commander, Burros decided one day to test his authority. Morgan had loaned the party his .45 pistol, and it hung in its Army holster in the middle room on the first floor. Well versed in cloak-and-daggering, Morgan had cunningly strung a yellow thread from the holster buckle to the gun tip. If the thread were broken, Morgan would know the gun had been tampered with. One day Morgan found the thread not only broken, but the gun gone—and in Burros' possession. Thoroughly affronted, Morgan threatened to remove the gun from headquarters, thus reducing substantially the armed strength of the party. Rockwell pleaded with him to reconsider. The gun crisis was finally resolved, with Burros the psychological victor. Morgan left the gun, contenting himself with a warning to Burros not to play with it: "It's a damned good gun and I would hate to lose it in court," he muttered.

In addition to such incidents as this, Rockwell's headquarters was periodically enlivened by a small stream of visitors—Nazi-minded men and women who came to talk with Rockwell and pledge him support. Support usually ended with the pledge and Rockwell was sure that some of his visitors were spies, from the police or the FBI or the Anti-Defamation League of B'Nai B'Rith, whose Washington office kept a close eye on the party. But he had no investigative facilities and had no way of knowing who the spies were.

Once in a while, foreign fascists would drop by—leaders of the National Socialist Fighting League of Malmö, Sweden, as well as British and Australian Nazis. But the visitors most important to Rockwell were the handful of men and women on whom he counted for money.

Money was in short supply in 1960 and every time the mail came Rockwell would rip open envelopes, shaking them out for currency. The bills piled up and the "troopers" contributed what they could toward expenses and toward Rockwell's salary—in the beginning thirty dollars a week. Rockwell began to say he would have to sell his Nazi souvenirs.

The American Nazi campaign, such as it was, was being run on little more than Rockwell's nerves and sometimes they snapped. One day he was so overwrought that he could not even bring himself to behave diplomatically to a woman who had made periodic financial contributions to the party. The woman took it upon herself to chide Rockwell for the violence of his anti-Semitic propaganda. Nobody doubted his ability, she told Rockwell, but wasn't he going a little far?

Rockwell looked at her mockingly: "Now let's not pretend that you're not in this just as deep as I am, that you are not just as dirty as I am," he said. And when the phone rang, proving to be another prankster, Rockwell, with one eye on his visitor, shouted into the mouthpiece: "Why you dirty, sneaky, cowardly stinking Jew, you miserable yellow streak, you'd better put back on your pink panties, you cowardly little queer."

"Now, Rockwell," the woman visitor remonstrated.

But Rockwell was, by now, beside himself. "I know you haven't heard that language before, have you?" he jeered. And, accompanying her to the door, he added, "Don't be ashamed to be seen with us big bad Nazis. Come on over again." As she drove away in her late model car, a trooper, who had witnessed the scene, said sadly, "There goes our money."

One day Rockwell was told that a Jewish reporter, a Nazi-taunter, had driven to the barracks in his Volkswagen. Rockwell leaped down the stairs. "Why, the sneaky little Jew, that ballsy little character, quick call the police on him, get out the rug, hurry."

A "rug" was tossed down on the doorway—an ark curtain from a synagogue. Rockwell spat upon it and ground the spittle into the cloth with his shoe. The Jew, a thin little man with a huge moustache, walked in.

"Look here," Rockwell said gleefully, "why don't you wipe your feet on this Jewish floor mat?" The troopers behind Rockwell doubled up with laughter.

The reporter had come to needle Rockwell. He suggested Rockwell call all his members together and have a convention—in a phone booth. Rockwell's rejoinders were largely limited to "That's what you think, that's what you think."

While the two were talking, a Rockwell man went to the phone and called the police to ticket the Volkswagen for illegal parking. When the reporter went out to get the ticket, the house was full of joy. Patler danced a jig with Braun, and

Rockwell stood on the steps, roaring. Tears rolled down their cheeks. "What a triumph!" Rockwell exulted. "That Jew got a ticket!'

The "troopers" always talked about "action" and "missions," which consisted principally of standing around in uniform and swastika armbands, looking for trouble while Rockwell spoke on the Mall. Rockwell made sure that the police knew in advance about his talks—for protection and to draw crowds and the press. Often he would call the Anti-Defamation League so they could have time to prepare a protest and so the word could get around to Jewish hecklers, which would mean more publicity.

Much of the time, Rockwell spent trying to patch up feuds—between Patler and Morgan, Burros and Ryan, between almost any two of the troopers. He walked a line between trying to calm down the troopers' enthusiasm—warning Patler, for instance, to go easy on propaganda among the Marines at Quantico lest he get into too much trouble—and whipping up the enthusiasm that flagged under the diet of Corn Flakes and water.

Now and then, he would give little inspirational talks. Looking at pictures of Hitler *Jugend,* Rockwell's voice would grow somber as he said he would spend a lifetime making up for the "murder of these German children."

"The Jews are through in seventy-two," he would say, parroting his slogan as if it had just occurred to him. Once he said: "When we reach absolute power all the top Jews will be tried in Jerusalem just like the Jews tried the Nazis in Nuremberg." One trooper had a compassionate thought: "The Jews may be the way they are because of environment. When we attain power we will start a scientifically controlled experiment. We will place a thousand or so Jews as babies into Gentile homes. We will let them grow up not knowing they are different. If they are big-nosed crooks by the time they are twenty-one, trying to get every dollar they can lay their hands on, we'll know. A Jew is a Jew is a Jew."

Burros thought this kind of talk was sentimental nonsense. He would fondle his bar of soap and shout that the only way was total extermination. One day a disturbed Jewish boy from Arlington showed up, said he wanted to help expiate the crimes of the Jews and become a member of the party. Rockwell and some of the others thought it would be a good publicity stunt to give the "Jew boy" probationary membership, but Burros was furious at the idea. No Jews! he insisted; the Jews would sully the purity of the movement.

There was no halfway with Burros as far as the Jews were concerned. Sometimes, to tease him, the troopers would say, "Burros, you look like a Jew boy yourself." He would fly into a rage and sulk until they told him they were kidding. And over and over, he repeated: "The Jews must suffer, the only way is that the Jews must suffer."

Burros was never terribly popular at the barracks. The troopers made fun of his queer waddling walk—and Rockwell called him the "ruptured duck." Warner called him a "human scissors" because of his habit of snatching up papers and documents to clip out Nazi pictures for his collection. He had a high, effeminate giggle that the troopers used to imitate.

The collection of Nazi material in Burros' suitcases grew —he found a mail order firm in California that specialized in Nazi souvenirs and bought medals and "Hitler *Jugend* knives." Burros had other collections, of spider pictures and of pornographic pictures. Once he cut out a picture of a nude in a girlie magazine, positioned a drawing of a swastika on her vagina, and asked Patler to take a photo and print it for him. Patler was indignant and Burros sulked for a while.

Burros went out on blind dates, but the troopers all believed that he couldn't "make it" except with prostitutes. Every now and then Burros would spend a weekend in New York and return with stories of his adventures with prostitutes.

Burros and one of the troopers had an arrangement one night—the trooper had picked up a girl and after he had finished with her would pass her on to Burros. The girl and the trooper spent a night in a car, but afterward he told Burros huffily that she was too nice to be passed around. Burros challenged him to a fist duel and the two stripped to their waists in the back yard and shuffled around each other for a few minutes.

Burros became a favorite target for practical jokes and at least one he loved himself. Rockwell was invited to a woman's house one night. He had never met her, but she said she was just dying to meet him. So Rockwell put on his best suit and dashed over. She turned out to be sloppy, fat, and ugly and Rockwell did not stay long.

When he returned to headquarters, he told Burros that this woman was a real beauty but that "we just don't have a man to match this woman's genius."

Burros volunteered immediately. "Let me do it, Commander." He begged Rockwell again and again and finally with a show of reluctance and admiration for Burros, Rockwell agreed.

Burros shaved, bathed, and went to see the woman. He didn't stay long either and when he returned he just laughed and laughed and said it was a wonderful gag the Commander had played on him.

The troopers sometimes mocked Burros but there never

was any doubt about his loyalty to the party or his usefulness. He was not only a printer but a "research specialist" on Jews. He told the troopers that he had learned Hebrew to be able to "investigate the enemy" better and on Saturdays a few of them would march down to the Library of Congress and watch Burros nonchalantly take notes from Hebrew books.

And, of course, Burros had earned his spurs. He had picketed the White House a half-dozen times and although Morgan thought he made a sloppy looking picketer with his waddle and slouch, everybody acknowledged that Burros was always ready for action.

Chapter Eight

On July 3, 1960, Burros took part in an action that brought about the arrest of seventeen party members, including himself, and led to Rockwell's commitment for psychiatric observation—a traumatic experience for all the American Nazis. The action was witnessed—indeed, participated in—by a reporter for the Washington *News* named George Clifford, who had "joined" the party shortly before, in order to write a first-hand account of its activities.

It began on a warm Sunday afternoon, when Rockwell was to deliver one of his typical addresses on the Mall. Rockwell climbed to his platform and Burros and the other troopers took up their positions in what Rockwell called his "circle of defense." (According to Clifford, there were "about twenty" of Rockwell's troopers present; according to Rockwell there were "by some stroke of fate only eleven . . . and one of these was a newspaper spy"; the figure of seventeen arrested was furnished by the police.)

The Nazi commander and his largely Jewish audience eyed each other, as Rockwell began, "My fellow Americans . . ." A chant from the audience drowned him out: "Sick sick sick sick . . ." Again Rockwell began, and again he was shouted down.

Rockwell sent Clifford to a park police lieutenant stationed on guard duty, to say he would not speak until the mob was quiet. The police lieutenant said he did not particularly care whether Rockwell spoke or not. At this point, according to Clifford, Rockwell sent a trooper through the ropes surrounding his platform, with instructions to "stir up the crowd," a fight started, and the trooper and his opponent both were arrested; Rockwell then encouraged J. V. Morgan to agitate the crowd a bit with a few rhetorical questions from the party repertory, such as: "Where did the Jews come from? They crossed a hound dog with a nigger." While Morgan was circulating—still according to Clifford—Rockwell screamed from his platform, "Jews, dirty Jews, filthy Jews"—and the crowd rushed him.

Rockwell's version (in a pamphlet) differs slightly from Clifford's.

"For an hour and a half . . . we tried our best to speak as we always had," he wrote, "but over two hundred and fifty Jew toughs and hoodlums put up such an unearthly roar of filthy insults and challenges to fight that I was never able to get past 'My fellow Americans.' We called for police again and again as we were spit on and hit with objects, but they stayed far out of operating range most of the time with folded arms. . . . Finally, when the Jews had worked themselves into a sufficient frenzy to be brave enough for two hundred and fifty of them to attack our eleven, they burst through the ropes and we had to fight desperately to survive." (Clifford, soon after the Mall fracas, dropped his disguise; in writing about Rockwell for his newspaper he described his own efforts to keep out the melee as inconspicuously as possible—"I fell down into a crouch and covered my head with my arms.")

Before the police could break up the fight and arrest the participants for disorderly conduct (at least half a dozen members of the audience were arrested along with the troopers), James Warner had been bitten in the ear, and Morgan had his face scratched from forehead to chin and ear to ear. Rockwell subsequently claimed (according to Clifford) that he had castrated a heckler with his bare hands. Burros and the others were bruised, but not seriously. (Rockwell's written account listed no physical damage inflicted on either side.)

In court to face disorderly conduct charges, Rockwell and his troopers heard Assistant Corporation Counsel Clark King suggest that Rockwell was not mentally competent to stand trial and that he should be committed for psychiatric observation. Burros, who vividly recalled his own scrutiny by Army psychiatrists, was more upset by this suggestion than any of the other troopers. He thought that if Rockwell were committed, he might be next. As for Rockwell, he was completely stunned. He was certain it was a Jewish plot to get him permanently out of the way. He requested a court-appointed lawyer and a three-week continuance of his case, both of which were granted.

Rockwell and his lawyer, O. B. Parker, spent the three weeks trying to arrange for legal evidence of Rockwell's sanity. It was not easy.

"We tried to find two Gentile psychiatrists to examine me," Rockwell later wrote. "NOT A SINGLE PSYCHIATRIST IN THE AREA WOULD EXAMINE ME AND TESTIFY! Finally I found one Irishman who would examine me and who gave me a letter as to my sanity, but that was not acceptable in Court, of course . . ."

Refusing to be "intimidated" by the pending court case against him, Rockwell continued to make public addresses. When his case came up on July 24, the suggestion again was made to have Rockwell committed for observation. Evidence of Rockwell's "probable" mental illness was presented before

Judge George D. Neilson, and he ordered a thirty-day commitment to the District of Columbia General Hospital for psychiatric observation.

Morale at the barracks plunged with Rockwell's removal. The more or less controlled hysteria with which the troopers managed to live while their leader was there to issue commands erupted into open panic. Burros in particular, idolizing Rockwell as he did, reacted to his absence with sullen shock. He lost heart even for a cherished project he had been working on—a tract describing his Army experience at Little Rock. (He never finished it.)

Burros believed, with the other troopers, that Rockwell's future was grim. Interestingly enough, these same men who accepted Rockwell's leadership with almost slavish obedience, had little faith in his ability to establish his sanity. Burros and the rest were concerned that Rockwell might not be released.

A number of troopers deserted and those who remained, including Burros, fell more and more into the pattern of bored, not-too-bright adolescents, suddenly abandoned by their parents. They slouched about the barracks, talked idly and halfheartedly about taking various forms of action to help their leader, bickered and taunted each other, frequently to the point of blows.

Rockwell's own gloominess about his future, on parting from his troopers, had been the chief cause of their depression. But, after his own initial shock, Rockwell hit on a plan for positive action (the difference, even in the shadow world of American fascism, between a leader and his followers).

It was this period of commitment that inspired Rockwell to issue his pamphlet, which he entitled "How to Get Out or Stay Out of the Insane Asylum." His view of what it was like in the "insane asylum" presented a fascinating contrast with the clinical report of the psychiatrists who examined him.

Rockwell was absolutely convinced that he was the victim of a Jewish conspiracy. In his hospital room at night he imagined "them" contriving evidence of his insanity and locking him away for life, or, even more horrifying, performing a frontal lobotomy. That "they" knew perfectly well he was not insane was beyond question. But proving his sanity in the face of their determination to prove his insanity was going to be a problem because, as Rockwell pointed out, "Psychiatry is notoriously Jewish, and . . . anybody who 'differs' in our regimented society is nuts.

"Since Negroes and Jews are obviously so lovable and valuable," Rockwell went on, "failure to perceive and appreciate and worship the superior qualities of these marvels of Nature is ipso facto evidence that the subject is a lunatic. And here I was, not only a man who professed a dislike of many Jews and a refusal to mix socially with Negroes, but who openly and scientifically planned to put large numbers of Jewish traitors in gas chambers, and get millions of Negroes to go back to their African home!"

Rockwell thought about this dilemma for a while, and then figured out an ingenious way of extricating himself. He was aware, in spite of his sarcastic use of the terms "lunatic" and "nuts," that paranoia was the medical term of his suspected condition, and he also knew that it was really the Jews, not he, who were paranoid. As he pointed out, "The major symptoms of paranoia are Delusions of Grandeur and Delusions of Persecution. For four thousand years these Jews have been ranting that they are 'God's CHOSEN people,'—a delusion which would get a single individual committed in a minute . . . and, at the same time, we are endlessly reminded, with pitiful wails, that 'Jews are persecuted,' they are always 'innocent scapegoats,' anti-Semitism is 'hate,'—etc., etc. These are clear-cut and inescapable proofs of paranoid tendencies."

That was step one; it was the Jews, not he, who were the true paranoids. He, however, was at their mercy because they had developed "a whole science—psychiatry," with which cunningly to subdue anyone who discovered who the real paranoids were; the way they worked their psychiatry was to pounce on their victims' least indication of what they could construe as antisocial behavior. Therefore, reasoned Rockwell, the only way to beat the psychiatrists at their own game was to "cooperate."

"Repugant as it may be," he wrote, "be friendly, popular with the coons, and make yourself liked by one and all." The second way to beat them was to be "honest"—which, by Rockwell's definition, was to avoid negative attitudes.

"When they ask you what you see in their inkblots and smears," he wrote, "gear yourself to see POSITIVE things and pleasant things—and tell them honestly. You will see in the blots what you are SET to look for. . . . Do not see blood, bodies, wreckage, etc.—but SET yourself to honestly see birds with handsome plummage, perhaps Japanese dancers with flowing robes, etc."

Rockwell's "cooperation" was, from his point of view, eminently successful. The psychiatrists concluded that he was legally "of sound mind, able to understand the charges against him and capable of assisting counsel in his own defense." They did, however, diagnose him as being a "paranoid personality."

From the psychiatrists' report:

Patient was asked why he is doing what he is doing & he replied that by nature, he sticks up for his ideals. Pt. said his present beliefs and actions started in 1951 when MacArthur was fired in Korea. Pt. wanted MacArthur elected president of U.S. A lady in California was giving a rally to support MacArthur but the rally never materialized. Pt. says the lady told him the Jews were to blame for stopping the rally. He then read an anti-Jew paper and was interested in the facts on the "Jewishness of Communism." He then read the paper's references and found that the Jewish Encyclopedia (that he found in the basement of the library) boasted of the Jews' part in Communism as did the *Manifesto* and *Mein Kampf*. Pt. states he is "not against Jews, but Communists and that most Jews are Communists and those that are not Communists are active in covering them up."

Pt. says he tried to have his views published but no one would publish them. He says *The New York Times* is "left wing" and similar to the *Daily Worker* in its writings.

Pt. states he is here "on principles." He states he could have forfeited his $10 bail but he will "fight 20 years" for his principles.

Pt. says he used Swastika for two reasons: one is to attract attention of the people because the people will not listen otherwise. He says "people are blasé and indifferent to principles." By this method he can "smash into their minds" his principles. Secondly, he used the Swastika as a symbol because it is the "symbol of the White Man." He says in reply to the question "Aren't Jews white men?" that Jews are not white men but are mostly a mixture with the Mongol race.

When asked what he thought of Hitler's mental status, pt. said that Hitler's writings are among the most brilliant in the world, and not mentally unbalanced.

Pt. said he decided to preach his doctrine because he felt like a man watching an orphanage burn down, in regard to Jews and Communism in U.S.A. Pt. states he is a man of much courage and strong will.

Adamantly, he states he is an American . . .

Responding to questions about his personal and family history, Rockwell gave the psychiatrists some revealing answers:

Pt. feels that as the oldest child, he had more responsibilities and less privileges than siblings. He resisted this and strenuously objected by "squawking" to his mother and father.

Pt. has been married twice. First at age 25 in 1943. His wife was then 28. His marriage lasted 10 years. Divorced by wife when he was in Iceland in 1953, on grounds of mental cruelty. He states that simply "she didn't like sea." He courted this wife three years. Married her because the most popular girl in school, pure and wholesome. He stated that before this marriage he was a "real dumb little jerk on sex, a virgin." He had three children during this marriage.

Pt. met his second wife in Iceland two months after divorce and had a "great time," with her. They married 6–7 months later. This wife is 12 years younger than pt. She had a previous marriage "to a drunkard." This marriage has given rise to four children. The family is all in Iceland now and pt. misses them very much.

Pt. stated he was authoritative with his children, but just. Pt. said his father was somewhat this way. This has resulted in his children loving the pt. and vice versa.

He stated that he had an authoritative aunt that he hated because she had no justice.

Among the significant incidents of his childhood, Rockwell listed the fact that he had "two very close friends in high school, one of whom was a Jew." He said this Jew must be much disturbed over his present actions. He said that he had lots of friends in youth.

Pt. stated that his biggest problem in childhood was being sheltered too much by his mother. . . . Mother made him

> wear shorts when other boys were wearing knickers, knickers when other boys were wearing pants, suspenders instead of a belt. He stated the children in school would rip off his shorts, etc.
>
> When asked what fights or aggressions he engaged in as a child, pt. replied: As a child he was able to figure out a law of gravity that made teachers angry and which pt. states was later discussed by Einstein. He stated he found a third method of proving the congruency of triangles that brought scorn from his teachers. He said his proof has subsequently been discovered by others.
>
> When asked if there were any situations that caused anxiety or troubles in his childhood, pt. replied that the wearing of unique clothes (as stated above) did cause him anxiety. . . .
>
> When asked if there was anything during his childhood which was particularly remarkable, the patient stated—"My mother was ignorant as to the wants and needs of a boy—she considered a pair of pants as a pair of pants and as you well know, there's more to it than that." He states that this was the biggest problem during childhood (the way mother dressed him, her not understanding boys, etc.)—He associates this with his not knowing much about sex prior to his first marriage. When asked how he solved this problem, the pt. stated that he "squawked" a lot about it and finally outgrew it, stating that the problem began when he was in the first grade and was resolved when he was in the fourth grade, but still associates this to his small knowledge of things sexual before and during his first marriage.

Among other random items, Rockwell volunteered the information that he was an agnostic, not an atheist; that the Negroes were being exploited and that their leaders were Jews and Communists.

The report noted that during the interview Rockwell "seemed relaxed."

> His conversation seemed to be that he was trying to convince interviewer of his opinions. It was noted that the pt.

had a reason for everything to the point of complete and broad rationalizations in which the reasons seemed to follow the action.

The Chief Psychiatrist's report said:

> I first wish to state that I do not personally approve the political philosophies Mr. Rockwell represents, nor can I condone his methods.
>
> From my examination and the observations of Mr. Rockwell in the hospital, I find him to be competent to stand trial. As to his diagnosis, in my opinion, he has a Paranoid Personality. This condition is well controlled at this time, and until he develops uncontrolled paranoid delusions and acts aggressively on those delusions outside of the law, I cannot testify that he requires hospitalization.
>
> His avowed intent at this time is to obtain publicity for his campaign. To bring in psychiatric testimony which may be construed as interference with his right of free speech and his removal from society because of a difference in political ideology will bring discredit to the psychiatric profession and will further Mr. Rockwell's cause.
>
> If Mr. Rockwell is the sick man I believe him to be, time and frustration will expose him. Let the Law handle him for breaches of the peace, inciting riots or treason as will probably be the case. I do not believe psychiatrists should be forced to determine what political philosophy the American people should hear or believe. This is, in my opinion, the peoples' choice in a democracy; it is not properly the psychiatrists'.

On August 3, 1960, a letter was sent to the criminal clerk's office, municipal court, from the psychiatric division of the hospital concerning Rockwell:

> This patient was admitted to the District of Columbia General Hospital on July 27, 1960.
>
> Psychiatric examination reveals Mr. Rockwell to be of

sound mind, able to understand the charges, and capable of assisting counsel in his own defense.

He may be returned to the court at any time.

In August, Rockwell stood trial, was found guilty of disorderly conduct and fined one hundred dollars.

Chapter Nine

Sometimes the phone would ring in the home of Jason Silverman in Bethesda, Maryland, and when the receiver was lifted there was a pause and then German music or the "Horst Wessel" song. Silverman's teen-age son would listen for a moment and then say:

"Come on, fella, lift it up, give it a go, go, go. Come on with that beatnik stuff, we love it."

It would happen sometimes that a voice would ask for Jason Silverman, a voice recognized by all members of the household. The son or Silverman's thirteen-year-old daughter would shout in a loud voice to Silverman:

"Daddy, here's that man calling you again, old Rockhead."

When Silverman would pick up the phone, Rockwell would say, "Hello, Jase?" and then tell him where the Nazi band planned to picket, or parade, or where the Commander would give his next speech.

For Rockwell's band, the enemy in Washington is not the Arlington or Washington police or the FBI. Rockwell likes to boast that the "cops are with us," and takes infinite pains to portray himself as a friend of the police. He notifies the police and the FBI of most of his planned activities, sends them logs of his visitors and files with them information on his members. There are several motives—to get police protection and through a police guard to increase the drama and dignity of his appearances, and to cloak the actions of the party in the trappings of obedience to law, in case of court action against him.

There is no evidence that the police reciprocate this feeling of comradeliness, and Rockwell never knows whether any given member is a true-blue Nazi and Jew-hater or a plant of the FBI.

But at Nazi headquarters the real enemy, the most cherished target, is the Anti-Defamation League of B'Nai B'Rith and its chief investigator and Nazi-watcher, Jason Silverman.

The growth and changes of the Anti-Defamation League reflect some of the growth and changes in the attitudes of American Jews toward anti-Semitism. The League was set up in 1913 by the Independent Order of B'Nai B'Rith, a Jewish fraternal society, with a budget of two hundred dollars and two desks in the Chicago office of Sigmund Livingston, a Jewish lawyer. Its object was to stop the defamation of the Jewish people by law and appeals to reason and conscience.

The waves of immigration of the late nineteenth century, bringing to the United States many Christians with the built-in anti-Semitism of the Old World, and the strange ways and manners of eastern European Jews, were producing new symptoms of anti-Semitism that frightened Jews who lived in the United States.

Harry E. Schultz, in a history of the League called *Not the Work of a Day,* writes: "In its early years, ADL's primary concern was the protection of American Jews from unfounded public calumny; this was accomplished by the personal intervention of important Jewish personalities who tactfully pleaded the cause of tolerance."

In its first stages, the ADL sought censorship legislation against books or plays or periodicals spreading anti-Semitism. Later, the ADL came to realize, as Schultz puts it "that the cure was worse than the disease." ADL came to oppose censorship and its activities widened—not only to deal with all forms of anti-Semitism and conduct attacks against them but, in the belief that liberties were indivisible, to protect the rights of Jews by fighting for the rights of all minorities. It became a broad-based civil libertarian organization, but its focus, of course, remained the fight against anti-Semitism.

The ADL has been involved in struggles against Henry Ford, whose anti-Semitism was a trauma to most American Jews, and against Father Charles E. Coughlin, the radio orator. And most particularly it has become a kind of centralized "private eye" watching the activities of people like Rockwell, whom Hitler taught it not to dismiss out of hand. Perhaps more than any other organization in the United States, the ADL is aware that private aberration can become public calamity.

Silverman, a tweedy, pipe-smoking attorney who was born in Boston in 1915, became quite intimately acquainted with Nazis and anti-Semitism during World War II. After serving with the Army in Australia, he became one of a group of officers selected to interview Nazi prisoners held at Fort Robinson in Nebraska. The purpose of the program was to try to probe for causes and motivations of Nazism in the German soldier, to find out "how he ticked," and the goal was to mine enough information to develop some kind of "reorientation program" for the end of the war.

The first manifestation of anti-Semitism Captain Silverman discovered in Nebraska was among his American fellow officers. Silverman and his wife were the only Jews on the post and they found that despite all their observances of military amenities—the calls on the wives of higher ranking officers, the cards left on the trays—they never were invited to post parties. Most Jews draw wounded into their shells at this kind of social anti-Semitism. Silverman asked to be heard at a post officer's meeting and proceeded to criticize his fellow officers politely but pointedly. Life became a bit more social for the Silvermans, principally because a report of his talk was forwarded to Army headquarters in Washington.

Silverman never did find out exactly what made Nazi German soldiers tick. He did find out some other interesting things, however—that anti-Nazi soldiers were beaten and sometimes murdered by the prisoners' own Gestapo and that when pictures of the mounds of dead at concentration camps were shown to the prisoners the reaction was that the dead were not Jews or foreign prisoners of the Germans at all but good Germans murdered by the Allies.

Ever since January, 1946, Silverman has been working for the ADL's investigation office. The boys at Rockwell's headquarters talk of him often, speculate about his files and his undercover agents, and love to plot little nuisance forays against him or the ADL. Rockwell hugs the idea that by calling "Jase" and letting him know of the Nazi activities, he gets "the Jews worked up" to the point where they give him publicity by taking action against him. Silverman, of course, lives with the awareness that the job of the ADL sometimes does indeed bring publicity to Rockwell and every decision to fight him has to be weighed against that.

Between "Jase" and the boys in the barracks there is something of the relationship between the police precinct captain and local small-time crooks. He knows them all by background and record, knows their weaknesses and fetishes, the girls they go out with and the postitutes they frequent. The Nazis know he knows and they have an admiration for his toughness, again not reciprocated.

Only very occasionally is there any person-to-person contact. Silverman once drove out to the barracks to look around. The Nazis recognized him—they have his picture and he has all of theirs—and called, "Hi, Silverman" as he strolled about. There were none of the usual anti-Semitic epithets that greet the occasional Jew walking around outside the barracks.

Silverman attends some of the court hearings against Rockwell, and in September, 1961, the two men got into a little fracas. Rockwell was in domestic relations court in Arlington to answer a proposed contempt proceeding for failure to keep up with his alimony payments to his first wife. Silverman was in the courtroom to see what clues might be available as to the amount of money Rockwell was getting, since Rockwell was paying alimony out of contributions to the party.

After the hearing, Silverman lingered in the back of the courtroom to talk to a reporter from the *Washington Evening Star*. As they came out of the courtroom into a long corridor, Silverman was spotted by Rockwell and about sixteen of his band. They were gathered at the end of the corridor Silverman had to approach to get to the parking lot and it was plain they were waiting to see what he would do.

Silverman started toward them and as he approached, Rockwell smiled, huddled briefly with his boys, who then formed a cordon across the corridor, shoulder to shoulder, blocking the door.

Silverman kept moving toward them and Rockwell shouted an about-face. The men wheeled, backs to Silverman, apparently so they could claim that they were just minding their own business. Silverman kept going, shoving his way past Rockwell and one of his squad, who dropped to the ground. Silverman kept going and outside the courthouse, the trooper who had dropped, took off his jacket, handed it to another trooper, and said, "Okay, here's where we have it out."

The gang had gathered and Silverman offered to take them on one at a time. Rockwell rushed up, pulled back the trooper squaring off, and jumped up and down with glee.

"We got him, we got him, we got the Jew bastard. We got him where we want him. He's assaulted him. We've got him for assault and battery."

The group hustled across the street into the complaint bureau of the police station, rushed up to the desk, and announced that they wanted to file a complaint against Silverman.

Silverman followed, waited until the Nazis had finished and the clerk had taken the information down on the complaint sheet. Then Silverman said he wanted to file a separate complaint on the same sheet, so that the sheet would show that seventeen Nazis accused one Jew of assault and one Jew complained against seventeen Nazis.

Rockwell stared impassively for a while at Silverman, then smiled briefly. He huddled again with his boys, then said to the clerk: "Tear it up," and they all marched out of the police station.

In his first months with the Nazis, Burros had listened to a great deal of Silverman and ADL talk in the barracks. The idea seized him to go right into enemy camp and he was convinced that this would make his name.

On the afternoon of July 26th—the day before Rockwell was committed for psychiatric observation—Burros and Patler entered the ADL headquarters at 1640 Rhode Island Avenue in Washington, walked up to June Zidek, the receptionist-switchboard operator, and asked if they could have the latest copies of the ADL bulletin. She told them they might find them on the fourth floor and the two men took the elevator up.

On the fourth floor they walked to the desk of Rose Gordon, executive assistant to Jason Silverman, who recognized them immediately from having seen them at picket lines and rallies of the Nazi party and from their pictures on file at the ADL. She told them she did not have copies of the bulletin for them and they left. She pressed the button for the elevator to return, to make sure they had left the building. In the elevator she found stickers, red, white, and black, with a swastika and the words: "We are back."

The next day Patler and Burros were on picket duty outside the White House carrying signs protesting the order for a sanity hearing for Rockwell: "If you don't love Jews and Niggers, you're nuts," and "Free Speech for Nazis." A police officer watched them picket, for seven hours. When they were finished, he put his hand on their shoulders and told them they were under arrest, on a charge by the ADL accusing them of defacement of property. Patler was furious because the officer had let them picket until their feet were sore before arresting them.

Burros and Patler were locked up pending arrangement of bail, and as the hours dragged on, Burros worked himself into a fury. He told Patler he was scared, scared that they would lock him up forever if he had to face a sanity hearing himself, and scared and furious that the party had deserted him.

Burros paced back and forth in his cell, cursing, shaking his fists, threatening to turn Rockwell and the party over to the Department of Justice, swearing he would never return to the party because they had betrayed him.

There was a drunk arrested for disorderly conduct in the next cell and the boys whiled away the time by having some fun with him. They told him all he had to do was to bang on the walls and he would be freed. When that didn't work, Burros told the drunk to take off his clothes and burn them. The drunk thought that was a good idea and when the guards came in to hose him down, the boys just laughed and laughed.

Patler's pregnant wife showed up about midnight and after giving her husband a piece of her mind arranged bail through a Jewish bailiff.

The case came before Judge Milton S. Kronheim on September 20, 1960, and both men entered pleas of not guilty. The judge was a member of B'Nai B'Rith and he asked James Jones, the court-appointed lawyer, if he had any objections to his trying the case. Mr. Jones said that the judge had always been fair and he had no objections. (Mr. Jones received an anonymous call assuring him that there was money behind the boys and he would be paid; he never was.)

The trial lasted a few hours and the defense tried to establish that someone other than Patler or Burros could have pasted the swastikas in the elevator. Burros took the stand to deliver the crucial testimony. He said that he had seen similar stickers at Nazi headquarters and himself had given one to a child outside the courtroom. He said he took it back "because I decided it wouldn't be good to leave it with a minor."

Q. Then you do carry them in your pockets?
A. On occasion I have, yes.
Q. And on this occasion were you carrying them in your pocket?
A. (Following a pause) Ahh, no sir; I didn't.

Q. Are you certain?
A. Well, it might have been stuffed in my wallet but as far as I know I didn't have any in my possession.

The jury took twenty minutes to find them both guilty and the judge called them before the bench. He asked them whether they had ever been in a mental institution. Patler said no and Burros said:

"Well, sir, I was, in service. Your Honor, I was declared of sound mind."

The judge said, "Well, I don't think there is enough indication here to send you down for mental observation, but you ought to be more careful."

The judge added a brief lecture:

"Well, you are both misguided. Let me try to explain something to you. Under our system, if anybody has done anything wrong you can make a complaint. If you think there's something wrong with the system, you have the right to petition to Congress, but you can't take it into your own hands to attack a group. It's that simple. Now I get the impression you are misguided."

Judge Kronheim asked Burros what the cirmumstances were under which he was sent to the mental hospital.

"Well," said Burros, "my national socialist beliefs became known in the Army and they sent me to observation to see if there was anything mentally wrong with me."

The sentence was one hundred dollars or ten days, and six months, suspended. The two men paid the fine and Patler filed an appeal, rejected by the Municipal Court of Appeals for the District of Columbia.

Burros did not appeal, but he loved telling and retelling the story of how he had gone into enemy camp and had confronted the Jews right in their own den and how he had been imprisoned and convicted for the cause.

The ADL and Silverman did not worry much about the great sticker raid. Their principal concern in relation to Rockwell is and always has been over the question of free speech—whether he should be allowed to make his public denunciations of Jews and "niggers." This is a debate that fascinates not only Rockwell and Silverman but a number of civil libertarians, who believe that there is more to lose by silencing Rockwell than by allowing him to talk. They believe that the damage to the cause of civil liberties would be greater than any damage Rockwell could do, and the Nazis, fully conversant with this attitude, know the names of every civil liberties lawyer and organization they can count on to defend them in court.

The position of the ADL and Silverman, unlike that of, for example, the American Civil Liberties Union, is that Rockwell and his band are not entitled to the protection of constitutional guarantees of free speech because their talks and propaganda are calculated to insult and damage others and thus cause disturbance.

Silverman puts the argument this way:

"It's very clear that the messages on picket signs, the methods and dissertations of public speakers and the circumstances of the meetings, when they are gross and explosive, when they use insulting or fighting words, do not entitle them to the protection of the First Amendment.

"This was stated with great clarity by the late Justice Murphy and a unanimous Court in the case of Chaplinsky versus New Hampshire, 315 U.S. 568, where a defendant had been convicted on a breach of the peace for calling a policeman a 'goddamn racketeer and damned fascist' under a statute which is very similar to a District of Columbia statute, which makes it an offense to address any 'offensive derisive or annoying word' to any other person in a public place.

"The Court said: 'There are certain well-defined and narrowly limited classes of speech, the prevention and punishment of which have never been thought to raise any constitutional problem. These include the lewd and obscene, the profane, the libelous and the insulting or "fighting" words, those which by their very utterance inflict injury or tend to incite an immediate breach of the peace.'

"Now the true test, any reasonable man would say, is that when a speaker makes certain utterances, if the utterances are such that it so exercises the subject or the listener against whom the utterance is made, that this subject will turn on the speaker and a breach of the peace will be committed or a riot might ensue, then the speaker has gone beyond the pale in terms of the constitutional guarantee."

Silverman believes that often the police "guard of honor" prevents the injured listener from striking back.

"So we have thus provided a balance on the scale in favor of Rockwell and against the public interest because the insulted person cannot react under a normal and reasonable circumstance. All of this of course plays in favor of Rockwell; he understands this, he knows this, and he relies on it heavily."

The ADL prepared a brief following the lines of the Chaplinsky case, won agreement from the District authorities. Orders were about to be mimeographed on January 21,1960, instructing the police to arrest Rockwell if he used insulting or "fighting" language. Other Jewish civil libertarians, however, protested and argued in favor of Rockwell's right to speak, and the authorities decided that they did not want to be caught in the middle and canceled the orders.

The policy in Washington now is that the patrolman has to act as an ad hoc constitutional lawyer, watching to see if the Nazis or the audience do anything that might result in a breach of the peace. On one occasion, police arrested an angry man who merely shouted at Rockwell, "What about Hitler?"

The ADL contention is that Rockwell's speeches and writings, his constant repetition that "traitors" will be exterminated, his own statements saying that the Jews must be "provoked and aggravated" beyond endurance, his award of "prison medals" to violators of the law, make it clear that his objective is violent action.

"The hell with park, post office boxes and private meetings," he wrote in one of his pamphlets. "The Jews and Reds and race mixers are on the march. They are out in the streets. If the white race is to survive, the monster must not be talked about or written about. It must be killed. Smash it. Crush it. Kill it."

"The nub of the problem," Silverman argues, "is that the civil liberties people don't look back into Rockwell's writings, his tirades, his preparation in advance of the affair, particularly the injunctions, the instructions he gives to his troopers to move up to the line of illegality. And in the mumbo jumbo, oftentimes undisciplined kind of housekeeping that prevails in the Nazi party, more often than not these troopers not only come up to the line but they very often go beyond the line, go over it."

Where the police do not cooperate by providing protection, Rockwell sometimes decides the better part of valor is to skip the demonstration. In a midwestern city he called the police, told them of his plans for a demonstration, and asked them what they planned to do. Not a thing, Rockwell was told; if he wanted to speak peacefully, go right ahead. What about protection, Rockwell wanted to know. The police said that if and when someone sought to restrain him or attack him, all he had to do was what every other citizen could do—call the police. Rockwell changed his mind and canceled the meeting.

Chapter Ten

The boys in the barracks came from different parts of the country, but they had a number of things in common. They were mostly of lower middle class backgrounds. They loved to shine their boots and use their fists. And sooner or later, most of them were seized with the idea that anything Rockwell could do they could do better. Rockwell insisted on being called the Commander, but he was known privately in the barracks by other names—the "wino" when he was drinking, Der Adolf, and sometimes when morale was not at its highest, simply as "the jerk." Disloyalty, however, was usually in direct ratio to lack of funds and the amount of Corn Flakes and water on the menu.

But since Rockwell had a way of finding a dollar at the right time, since he was able to command the publicity that the troopers craved, and particularly since he was able to exert the mastery that they also craved, the bouts of disloyalty were usually subdued and often followed by periods of euphoria and even ecstasy. However, in most of the troopers there lived the fond thought that perhaps he, not Rockwell, was destiny's man, and the turnover in the little propaganda shop was considerable.

Dan Burros might have felt privately that he, too, had it in him to be a leader, but if so he kept the thought to himself.

Dan Burros rose in rank and responsibility and Dan Burros enjoyed himself.

He even managed, for a month or so, to combine the exhilarating if Spartan militarism of barracks life with a certain amount of creature comfort not to be found within the Arlington compound. At the beginning of 1961 he was still working for the Chamber of Commerce in Washington and he felt he could afford the luxury of living quarters that were within easy commuting distance of his job, while still within comfortable traveling distance of the barracks. With two of his fellow troopers, Ray Schultz and Ralph Grandinetti, Burros moved into a rooming house at 2933 28th Street, N.W., near the Shoreham Hotel—a quiet, tree-lined street in an eminently respectable neighborhood.

The house was owned by a widow, Mrs. Mary Strattos, who lived there with her daughter, also named Mary. Burros, Schultz, and Grandinetti moved into the basement apartment, which Mrs. Strattos had advertised in a newspaper. They paid seventy-five dollars for the apartment, which had its own entrance.

The three troopers quickly made themselves cozy in the apartment—they stocked their larder with coffee and canned food (not gourmet fare, but compared with the meager menus of the barracks, *cordon bleu*), they unpacked their Nazi books and pamphlets, their phonograph and German records, and hung a three-by-four-foot photograph of Hitler on the wall.

It was not long before Mrs. Strattos began to regret having accepted them as tenants. Shocked and offended by the portrait of Hitler the first time she was confronted by it, she turned it to the wall. Burros promptly turned it back. A day or two later, Mrs. Strattos again turned it to the wall. Again Burros turned it back.

Mrs. Strattos' daughter, who was also growing annoyed with the new tenants because they had a habit of playing German marches at full volume in the evenings when she had guests, recalled that both she and her mother decided they had made a bad bargain.

"Whenever Mother went downstairs to take out the trash or do the washing," she said, "she would find that picture facing her. She would turn it around to the wall, then later Burros would turn it back again. It was really quite ludicrous, like two children playing at who would get the last licks."

The confrontation Mrs. Strattos finally had with Burros was not ludicrous, however. Mrs. Strattos was frightened. According to her daughter:

"Mother told me at dinner one evening that Burros seemed to be quite angry and very mean looking. She was frightened by his looks and by his face." Her fear did not prevent her, finally, from pulling down the picture, nail and all. She wanted him to go. And soon after—near the end of February—he did. He had been fired from his Chamber of Commerce job and could no longer afford the rent. The Strattoses did not know that, of course. They recalled, simply, that all three troopers "left very suddenly and without notice of any sort."

Burros moved back to the barracks. He was now completely dependent, financially, on the Nazi party. Although he had no one but himself to blame for being fired from his Chamber of Commerce job, his loss of income was something of a blow.

On February 20, the word had got around to the executives of the Chamber of Commerce that their multilith operator was doing and saying some strange things.

Leonard Tillet, the production supervisor, was told by

some of the other young men that Burros was trying to get his fellow workers to join the American Nazi Party. As one of the youngsters put it: "Burros is giving us a lot of crap about the Nazis."

Tillet notified his superiors who called Burros into the office immediately.

"Are you a member of the Nazi party?"

"Yes, I am proud of it."

The executives made it clear that however proud Burros might be of the Nazis, they did not share that emotion and that he was through.

"Do you mean you are going to fire me? We will have to picket."

The executives said they would have to bear up under that and Burros left, clicking his heels and heiling Hitler at the door. He returned to his locker, got out a Nazi swastika armband, and walked out.

Burros and a gang of other troopers did picket, handing out leaflets accusing the Chamber of Commerce of hypocrisy and quoting executives as saying (which they have denied) that they approved of Nazi aims but did not like the "methods." The Chamber of Commerce says it never would have hired Burros if it had known of his political background. (A sufferer in the episode was the employment agency that sent Burros to the chamber; since he worked there less than a year the agency did not collect a fee from the chamber.)

Back at the barracks, Burros made the most of being a full-time Nazi.

Much of the time he slouched around the barracks in old clothes but whenever a camera appeared for the inevitable group photographs, Burros rushed upstairs to wash and comb and get out his uniform. He and Patler were the uniform committee and Burros spent long happy hours sketching new uniforms and decorations.

He adored all the little fraternitylike trappings that went with being a trooper, like the Nazi knock for entrance to headquarters—two slow, three quick—and the way the boys would drive around town sometimes sounding the rhythm on their car horns.

The White House picketing was great fun, too. A young man named Roy Frankhouser visited headquarters on an "inspection" trip as an officer of the Citizens' Council of America and stayed to take part in some of the fun and games. He found Burros full of enthusiasm and joy. Frankhouser found himself passing out literature—"Gas Communist Traitors"—in front of the White House. Sweat was dripping from Frankhouser's face, but Burros was jovial about the whole thing. "It's wonderful, it's wonderful," he assured Frankhouser. "You'll enjoy this, it's a great thing. Assure you the rights of freedom of speech."

Burros wasn't much for exercise, but he did like the drill and the salutes and once he enrolled in a karate class. For a couple of weeks he went around slapping one hand against the other and chopping at boards. That resulted in a broken bone rather than a broken board and Burros dropped karate.

Burros loved guard duty at Rockwell's rallies and stared happily into the television camera, holding signs or a swastika on a stick or standing fiercely with arms folded. And most particularly Burros loved the titles that came his way and the intrafraternity publicity that went with them. He became "Lieutenant Dan Burros, National Secretary." That was in July, 1961, and Burros was considered third ranking man at headquarters, just behind Morgan and the Commander himself. Then his picture appeared again in the bulletin as "political education officer."

Burros was still expected to concentrate on printing, but he was able to parlay his trade and his rank, writing and producing *The Official Storm Troopers' Manual* as Lieutenant Dan Burros, political education officer. (Layout and design by John Patler, who rewarded himself with a picture on the inside back cover.)

Burros' own picture appeared on the first page of the twelve-page booklet, just above the dedication to Horst Wessel, "who fell for his race and nation, murdered by Jew-Communists on the 23rd of February, 1930, in the original struggle of the White Race in Germany." Burros' private copy of this literary work bore his rubber stamp—name, party rank, and eagle with swastika.

The style was Talmudic. Why are we nationalists? Why are we socialists? How do we differ from the Marxists? From the socialists? The philosophy was Rockwell's—death to all traitors, beat the Jews at their own game:

> Struggle is an elemental part of nature. Without struggle civilizations wither and die. To remain young and virile, civilizations must be watered by blood and tears. . . .
>
> Why do we advocate gas chambers for traitors? The extent of traitors' conspiracy requires a large scale method of execution. Also the tradition exemplified by gas chambers drives traitors frantic and helps expose them. . . .
>
> One of the great jokes of modern times is the way National Socialists utilize the institutions of liberalism to destroy said institutions. An example is our "use" of the American Civil Liberties Union. The ACLU is forced to give us legal aid. If they do not help us it makes it apparent that they are only interested in defending the "liberties" of left-wing groups. The sword with which we smite the ACLU is double-edged. Firstly they have to give legal aid to Nazis whom they hate and secondly they lose much support. A good deal of their contributions come from Jews. It can be well imagined that

> Jews do not relish paying legal fees for Nazis. Therefore contributions to the ACLU drop.
>
> Mass psychology. The mass is decidely feminine. They admire strength and force. The masses say no, but what they mean is force me to say yes to what I really want but won't admit.

And about the "Jewish motivation":

> The startling answer to the Jewish enigma is that the Jews are insane. The Jews as a race are *paranoid.* This sick people must be stopped before they drag the world down with them.

The leaflets and the pamphlets kept coming out, and there was great joy in the barracks when a new $1,200 press arrived. The new press made Burros even more important.

Aside from the printing and picketing and writing and drilling there were little expeditions for Burros to enjoy—like the "Hate Bus" mission. That was in May of 1961 when the Negro Freedom Riders were in the news.

Rockwell sent out a Volkswagen bus loaded with troopers and propaganda to New Orleans to "symbolize the fact that decent Americans do hate and should hate Communism and race-mixing."

The expedition was not entirely Rockwell's inspiration. In March of 1961 an English fascist named Michael Slatter, who headed a little Nazi cell in New Orleans, visited headquarters and told Rockwell that he could raise some money to finance a Nazi expedition to New Orleans. Rockwell then hit on the "Hate Bus" idea, sent telegrams to the governors of several southern states demanding protection, and called Silverman to urge him to "push the publicity button."

Burros was part of the expedition, but he did not have a full share of the fun. In New Orleans, Patler and Burros drew straws to see who would stay in the hotel room to keep in contact with Washington headquarters and the New Orleans cell. Burros lost and was doomed to the hotel room.

Burros sat in the hotel room, hungry and on the verge of tears, while the troopers were hustled off to jail after demonstrating. Morgan sent one hundred and fifty dollars to Burros to help the troopers. Burros picked up the money at Western Union.

As he entered the building—followed by a police tail—a New Orleans Nazi sidled up to him. The two men managed to dodge the police and Burros gave the New Orleans contact the money; in return he got a meal in the contact's house. But the mission ended glumly for Burros. The police found him again and then escorted him to the bus station and gave him the choice of getting out of town or going to jail. Burros chose travel.

The mission also ended sourly for Rockwell. The New Orleans boys spent most of their time indoors on orders of the police and the local Führer got into a spat with Rockwell, accusing him of raiding his personnel. Rockwell then "washed his hands" of the New Orleans outfit, known as NSRP (National States Rights Party). He ordered a couple of his troopers who belonged to the NSRP to quit the New Orleans group or get out of the Nazi party. Morgan described Rockwell's chat about the iniquities of the New Orleans group as the "damnedest ass-chewing I ever heard." A couple of the Rockwell boys did quit, the court proceedings in New Orleans drained the treasury, and the party emerged from the adventure of the "Hate Bus" financially weakened and politically shaken.

But there were counterbalancing triumphs. Money was found for a bigger barracks on Wilson Boulevard (Burros stayed at North Randolph Street because of the printing operation there) and Rockwell organized an economic enterprise. It was called "Homestead Builders" and the idea was to put idle troopers to work making money for the party. They bid low on work like lawn maintenance and house painting. Not all the boys enjoyed it; they called the operation the "Slavestead Company."

At headquarters, Burros was known as one of Rockwell's most soulful admirers; one of the troopers said he was the kind who "would ask Rockwell before he goes to the toilet." He worked hard at the printing assignments and liked to relax by gazing at an oil portrait of himself hung over his cot. Painted by a friend, it showed Daniel Burros, standing rigidly at attention, in German storm-trooper uniform. Behind him rose the chimneys of Auschwitz.

Burros also liked to dream up special missions he thought would bring publicity. One day Burros volunteered to take six other troopers and parachute over New Jersey, waving Nazi flags on the way down. Rockwell did not think much of the idea.

Burros, as a high ranking and trusted aide of the Commander, accompanied him on what Rockwell considered one of his most important expeditions—attendance at a Black Muslim rally in Washington.

Rockwell's propaganda and talk is full of "niggers," whom the party members all consider a subhuman species. But Rockwell became enchanted with the idea that the Black Muslims wanted exactly what he wanted, separation of the races, and felt they would make interesting allies against the Jews, as well as supplying him with a beguiling propaganda platform.

On the afternoon of June 25, 1961, a Sunday, Burros went with Rockwell and a couple of other American Nazis to the Uline Arena in Washington for a Black Muslim rally. They were all enormously impressed with the Black Muslims—with the vendors making money for the movement by selling Black Muslim souvenirs and periodicals, with the convoys of chartered buses from all over the country, with the stern looking Fruit of Islam guards. They were also impressed with the efficient frisking they received when they entered, the constant inspection and surveillance of the arena, and the presence of TV crews.

A Muslim guard called George greeted Rockwell, whispered over his walkie-talkie that the "big man was coming now," and escorted the Nazis to seats of honor—unfortunately just out of range of the TV cameras. Negro journalists rushed over to Rockwell, who assured them he regarded the Black Muslims as good "black Nazis."

"I am fully in concert with their program and I have the highest respect for Mr. Elijah Muhammed," he announced.

He told a touching story of how he came to be anti-Semitic —it seemed there was a Jewish bully at his school who picked on all the little kids.

Rockwell said the only real difference between himself and the Black Muslims was a matter of territory—"they want a chunk of America and I perfer that they go to Africa." A bit later he said that he might possibly promise Elijah Muhammed Mexico if he wanted it although the border problem might require some thought.

Burros and Rockwell sat entranced at the professionalism of the decoration and stagecraft, at the enthusiastic but disciplined cheering, at the way the guards held their position and posture despite the suffocating heat in the arena.

Then came a high point of the meeting—the appearance of Malcolm X, who played the emotional keys of the audience like a piano. Midway in his speech, Malcolm began his demand for donations—"I don't want to hear clinking, I want to hear that soft rustle."

Malcolm called first for donations of one hundred dollars, got three, dropped to fifty dollars with no takers, and then came down to twenty dollars. At that point, Rockwell grimly got out his wallet, pulled out a twenty-dollar bill, and gave it to a Fruit of Islam man to be sent up to Malcolm. When Malcolm asked who had donated it, a Rockwell trooper shouted, "George Lincoln Rockwell," and the reporters and cameramen swarmed around the Commander. At Malcolm's suggestion, Rockwell stood to applause and Malcolm said, "I'll bet that's the most applause you ever received in all your life." Rockwell was not enormously amused, but managed a thin smile.

One of Elijah Muhammed's disciples took the stand and although the audience began trickling out, Rockwell and his boys stayed to applaud the speaker's denunciations of the Jews. Elijah Muhammed never showed up, but as consolation Rockwell was interviewed by a TV reporter outside the arena. He told how he had been urged by many Black Muslims in the audience to make a speech, a quick bit of on-camera thinking, as nobody had approached Rockwell directly at all at the meeting.

Rockwell, in Chicago in 1962, appeared before another Black Muslim meeting and this time did speak, saying that Negroes had been getting a raw deal in America and that it was the fault of the Jews. As he ended, he and the ten Nazis he had brought with him gave the Nazi salute and heiled Hitler. In an issue of a Rockwell publication called *The Storm Trooper,* he reproduced a comment from Elijah in the April, 1962, issue of *Muhammed Speaks:*

> Mr. Rockwell (American Nazi Party) has spoken well. He has lived up to his name. He is not asking you and me to

> follow him. He endorsed the stand for self that you and I are taking. Why should not you applaud? No other white people want you to do such a thing. His own people will hurt him or try to hurt him, you heard what he said, just because they have taken a stand to see that you be separated to get justice and freedom. . . . What right have you to sit there and hold your hand when you know he is telling the truth. No, the trouble of it is you are scared to death! You don't want the white slave master to say "I heard that you were there listening and enjoying the German Nazis or the White Circle leader." What do we care if they are white? If they are speaking the truth for us, what do we care? We'll stand on our heads and applaud!

The barracks boys did not get much physical action that summer in 1961, but they did get a chance to take after some Jewish youngsters twice.

Some boys from Arlington had gone over to the North Randolph Street headquarters and were throwing stones at the buildings. The troopers spilled out, about six including Burros, and gave chase. Burros found himself running in one direction, the boys and the troopers in another. He stopped short, rushed back to the house, foraged around, and came down with a baseball bat. He never caught up with the youngsters, but some of the other troopers did and were hauled into court, where Burros was called to the stand as a witness. The judge questioned him closely about the baseball bat and Burros stuttered and stammered and finally told the judge: "I'm not, what do you call it, a psychoanalyst. I don't know why I had the baseball bat." One trooper, Anthony Edward Wells, was sentenced to sixty days in jail for assault and battery and two others were acquitted.

Eleven days earlier, on July 8, the troopers dragged three passing boys, one Jewish, into the barracks, handcuffed one of them and harangued them. The father of the Jewish boy, thirteen-year-old Ricky Farber, swore out complaints, and Richard Robert Braun and Robert Franklin Garber, the troopers, were tried for simple assault. They were convicted and sentenced to twelve months on the state road gang.

Burros testified during the trial that he had heard the boys talking as they passed headquarters and heard one of them say, "Look at that Nazi rag. We ought to tear it down." The boys maintained that they had not made such a remark.

But in that summer of 1961, affairs were not going well in the American Nazi Party. Nothing unusual had happened. Rockwell and his band lived in a manic-depressive atmosphere, of great glee over small victories and deep gloom over setbacks, which led to more feuding and more bickering and thick despair.

Rockwell was constantly talking about traitors and betrayal and fought with one or another of his troopers, who would in turn become a focus of discontent to whom the others would tell their gripes against the Commander and their comrades. When Rockwell saw three or four of the boys going out together he would become convinced that they were conspiring against him. Troopers arrived, were praised by Rockwell as real fighting Americans, left disillusioned and were denounced as Jew traitors, returned and were welcomed as real fighting Americans.

The Commander brooded a lot that summer, about the money mail he was not getting and the lunatic mail he was getting, as from the Californian who wrote that he had designed a ray gun which he poked through mail slots to disintegrate "Jewish spies." The Commander whispered to his boys that so-and-so was an FBI plant and that somebody else in their midst was an ADL spy. There was some justification in this, of course. Rockwell's hard-core membership was never more than about forty-four and of those forty-four a good number were anti-Rockwell undercover agents of one kind or another—from the police, other investigative bodies, or opposing fringe societies ferreting out his few little secrets—or newspapermen posing as Nazis while diligently gathering material for articles. The chief difficulty that the agents and writers faced was not Rockwell's security, which was virtually nonexistent, but simply keeping a straight face.

The Commander himself was not looking very well that summer. The party was getting nowhere, and money was hard to come by to pay the bills and meet the alimony payments. Rockwell slouched around headquarters unshaven, in an undershirt stained with food droppings, and complained of headaches and fatigue. He cut down on his public speaking and altogether seemed to be coming apart. Burros at first was sympathetic and sad and told other troopers that the master just did not seem himself anymore.

Then Burros began to wonder whether Rockwell ever really had been himself, the commanding Commander he had built in his mind to adore. Patler, by then Burros' closest friend, was also having his doubts about the inevitability of Rockwell's glorious destiny. (Much later, Patler would blame Burros for stirring up discontent and Burros would say Patler was the instigator of the complaints.) But the fact was that Burros, in spite of the exalted rank he had achieved in the party, was beginning to feel restless in the barracks. Though he had stuck it out longer than many of his fellow-troopers, he, too, was at last starting to experience the urge to break out on his own, to have a fling at leadership, of forming his own party.

Another trooper, Ralph Grandinetti, had already left with the idea of forming a new party in New York and Burros decided to make the break, too.

One More Victim

Quitting the American Nazi Party can be a rather sticky matter. Troopers do not enjoy the idea of marching up to Rockwell and just resigning. One or two have done that and the reaction was not pleasant enough to encourage others to face Rockwell that way. To Rockwell, anyone who left, however valued and praised he had been during his stay, instantly became a treacherous, cowardly rat. Mostly, defectors just pack up and leave by night, through a window, to avoid embarrassing conversations with the guard on night duty.

Burros chose the window, in the early morning of November 5, 1961. Before leaving, he thoughtfully removed some material from Rockwell's files, including a copy of his own party applications, and carefully packed all his Nazi pictures, clippings, decorations, knives, and his pornography and spider collections in a couple of suitcases. Burros then made his way to Patler's Washington apartment, and the next day he and Patler drove in Patler's car to New York, to form their own party and pursue their private glory.

Chapter Eleven

The magazine was John Patler's idea, but when Dan Burros heard the title he went into a kind of anguished ecstasy. He clasped his hands, begged Patler please, please to allow him to edit it. It fitted so well with his personality, he said, it was just what he wanted to work on; if only Patler would let him, he would find the money to print it, spend all his spare time on it. Patler thought it over a bit, smiled at his friend, and said all right.

The first issue was dated July, 1962. It was a tiny thing, four and a half inches by five and a half, printed in photo offset, sixteen pages. The back cover consisted of a hangman's noose and under it: "Impeach the TRAITOR John F. Kennedy for giving aid and comfort to enemies of the U.S.A."

The front cover was a photograph of Armand Belvisi being led away in handcuffs by French police after his arrest for plotting to kill President de Gaulle. Above the photograph was the title: *"Kill! Magazine* . . . dedicated to the annihilation of the enemies of the white people." Dan Burros, editor, signed the lead article: "The Importance of Killing."

The enemies of the white race would emasculate us by having us believe that our sound instincts are some horrible heresy called "racism" and any attempts of the white race to defend itself are called "murder" and "war crimes."

Let us cast aside notions that have been planted in our minds by a thorough system of brainwashing. Away with hypocrisies and lies! Let us face the truth!

Man is a killing organism! He must kill to survive. He must kill to advance. . . . The enemies of the white race have been trying to destroy it, by weakening the white man's will to fight (which of course means to kill). Let us rip aside this veil of lies and hypocrisy. . . . Let us show them who is the natural elite . . . who is the world's greatest killer!

White man! Unsheath your terrible sword! Slay your enemies. Kill! Kill! Kill! . . . White men! The American National Party offers you the leadership and organization you need. Join us, and regain your rightful birthright. We will build a mound of corpses of traitors from which you can glimpse the great future. Only through organization and attainment of political power can the traitors be annihilated on a grand legal scale.

The headquarters of the newly formed American National Party was far less prepossessing than even the mean barracks that served Rockwell in Virginia. It was a one-room wooden shanty at 97–15 190th Street in the section of Queens called Hollis. There were never more than about a half-dozen members—most of them "founders" and almost all with fine titles; John Patler was national chairman, Ralph Grandinetti was state chairman and national organizer, a man named Paul Dekal was "defense corps commander," and Dan Burros was national vice chairman. (The group's impact was nonexistent. On the rare occasions when it satisfied its primary goal of getting into the newspapers, Burros' name was often misspelled Burrows or Burroughs.)

Right-fringe "parties" like the American National Party

spring up and wither almost overnight. Most of these parties have the same core of members, and often these members belong to several simultaneously and swap membership cards as children swap marbles. The parties, while they last, exist largely in the imagination of the members, bolstered by little that is tangible except letterheads on the stationery, and then disappear with the first intraparty feud. The kid with the ball and bat walks out, and the baseball game is over.

These groups are, however, of some minor interest to students of the political right and to psychologists, and of considerably more than passing interest to the police.

Their major political interest clinically is their symbiotic or parasitic relationship to the left-wing groups. Little parties—clubs, really—like the American National Party have no real programs beyond a jargonized racist platform and one reads almost exactly like another. They have almost no money—Burros paid for most of the fifty dollars an issue it cost to have the four issues of *Kill!* printed in a downtown New York photo-offset plant—and no members whose names and backgrounds in themselves can win attention from press or radio.

To get attention, the American National Party, during its brief existence, had to feed off the activties of the left or off liberals and intellectuals. The left is identified with causes or controversies—Vietnam, Cuba, military service—that do command press attention. The intellectuals produce plays or movies that are noticed by the press.

Burros and Patler followed Rockwell's technique of keeping an eye out for any left or liberal meeting they could picket, any controversial play or movie they could denounce with sandwich boards. Burros would pore over the newspapers for word of a meeting or opening and when he could round up a few people, would appear, after having notified the newspapers. The little group spent a number of cheerful nights picketing theaters where "Exodus," the movie about Israel, was playing and Burros marched up and down outside the Brooks Atkinson Theatre at the opening of "The Deputy," a play about the role of Pope Pius XII during the German extermination of the Jews.

Most of the time, the newspapers ignored the picketers except for a word or two. The only assured way to break into print was to start enough rumpus to attract the police and perhaps get arrested. This was a delicate operation because Burros and his friends had to walk the thin line between attracting attention, which they craved, and getting into a fight, which they did not particularly crave.

But although newspaper clippings were relatively sparse, Burros and the others did find rich satisfaction in the club. They all lived in the same fantasy of being revolutionaries who would one day attain power and pay off their enemies, and each member both fed upon and fostered the others' dream. The club was their real world—the jobs they held (Burros worked in a Jewish-owned printing company, kept his thoughts to himself while on the job, and was generally regarded at the shop as a quiet, decent sort) were the sleepwalking dream.

Best of all, the party was *theirs*. They talked a lot about Rockwell, and drew venomous caricatures of him. Now, for a brief moment, they were *all* Rockwells, all masters, simply waiting for the arrival of the followers and servitors, which, they told each other, was inevitable.

In the meantime, pending that day, there were so many interesting things to do. There was the picketing and the swaggering appearances in court to pay off the disorderly conduct fines, but there was so much more.

For Burros, New York was a kind of collector's paradise. He would spend his Saturdays prowling around the tiny antique shops and secondhand stores of midtown and lower Manhattan, poring over bins of medals and souvenirs and books for memorabilia of the Nazis, spending whatever spare money he had for a picture, or a volume in German "exposing" the annihilation of the Jews as an Allied propaganda campaign. Sometimes he would find an Iron Cross or a Nazi decoration sold by a GI veteran and if he did not have enough money that Saturday he would beg the store owner—often Jewish—to lay it aside for him for next week.

Then there was Yorkville, the section in the east eighties of Manhattan famous for its German restaurants and delicacy stores, its German bookshops and travel agents and bars. Once it was almost entirely German-American, and it was on the streets of Yorkville that the German-American Bund held its pro-Nazi meetings before World War II.

The population of Yorkville has shifted considerably. Expensive high-rise buildings have replaced many of the smaller apartment houses and there are now probably more Jews than Germans in the neighborhood and it is as good a place to find bagels and smoked whitefish as it is to find Munich beer and liverwurst.

But it remains the sentimental mecca of the right-fringe. Burros neither smoked nor drank, but he spent most of his free evenings in the bars and restaurants of Yorkville. Everybody knew him and when he walked into one of his favorite hangouts, dressed in his black leather coat, he was at home.

There were always people around who would examine the odd bits of his collection that he kept in his pockets and wallet. There were toughs from the neighborhood and other parts of the city who would curse the Jews and talk about grabbing some Jew broad and giving her a gang shag. And from time to time, there were real heroes who would talk to Burros.

These were Germans who had served in the German Army and had migrated to the United States. They all claimed to be officers; to hear these men tell it, there wasn't a Yorkville veteran of the *Wehrmacht* who held a rank below that of lieutenant. These former officers listened to Burros talk of the glory of Hitler and of *Der Tag* in the United States, and none of them laughed at him. Sometimes they would give him pictures of their *Wehrmacht* or *Luftwaffe* days and these he treasured above all because they were the real thing.

The American National Party did not have enough money for uniforms, but Burros could satisfy himself in part at least by sketching the jodhpurs and tunics and belts and boots they would someday have. Talk of uniforms always excited Burros sexually. In Arlington, his occasional visits to prostitutes had usually coincided with some dress-up occasion—a barracks drill, or a picture-taking session. In New York, as a founder of his own party, able to initiate "policy meetings" about uniforms at will, his visits to prostitutes became more frequent. There were two or three he visited almost compulsively—and in at least one case, incautiously. He showed up one day at the apartment where Patler lived with his family, scratching himself, and said he had a chancre. Patler was indignant that Burros should come to a house with small children in such a condition.

Burros found other pleasurable ways to mark time in New York, pending the full blossoming of the American National Party. He had a variety of letterheads printed with his name, the swastika, the German eagle. There was the letterhead for the American National Party, a letterhead for a magazine he put out a couple of times called *The International Nazi*

Fascist. He had a richness of rubber stamps with eagle and swastika and he loved to decorate his letters with two or three of them. He signed them all off with *Heil Hitler* and often with *Judah Verrecke.* He loved to invent organizations and one of his favorites, for which he had a stamp made up, was the American Committee to Free Rudolf Hess. He printed his name in German type on his stationery and salted his letters with German phrases. In one letter to a former Rockwell trooper, enclosing his phone number, Burros cautioned the trooper to treat it as *Reichsgeheimache*—state secret.

Burros squirreled his collection away in several places in the city, places where he would spend the night. Sometimes he shared an apartment briefly with young Nazi comrades, occasionally he would sleep over at a friend's house and from time to time he rented a furnished room for himself. And often he would stay the night at his parents' home in Richmond Hill.

Almost never would Burros talk about his parents. But there were times when he would tell friends that his parents knew about his Nazi activities and connections but that he had them good and scared and although they would "yell" at him they would not dare try to stop him. George and Esther Burros did know that their son had become a Nazi and was devoting his life to preaching murder of the Jews.

Exactly what went on in the small apartment in Queens when Burros came to see his parents nobody knows but three people; the son is dead and the parents became too deeply steeped in their anguish to talk to outsiders. Dan Burros, of course, never hinted to his friends that his parents were Jewish; he simply said they did not agree with him and that he kept them cowed. People who knew the Burros couple believe that they thought their son was deeply ill and that it was their job to protect him as best they could; whether they ever tried to get psychiatric help for him is not known.

But it is known that Dan Burros could never tear himself completely away from his Jewishness. In hindsight it is quite obvious that he took deliberate risks that could have resulted in his being unmasked as a Jew.

The neighborhood was full of people who knew Burros as a Jew and had no idea that he had become a Nazi. But he always kept returning. There were times when old men of the congregation to which his grandfather had belonged, bearded Jews, would stop him on the street or subway platform and talk to him—"Danny, how have you been, and what's with your parents?"

Burros would answer politely and move on. He was always alone on those occasions and yet a half-dozen times he took Nazi comrades into the neighborhood. He would tell them to wait across the street while he visited his parents because they didn't like his friends. And yet he knew that every time he took a Nazi into the neighborhood he stood the risk of being greeted by an old Jew, or by the rabbi of the Congregation of the Sons of Israel, and thus exposed. Once when Roy Frankhouser was waiting for him a few blocks from his home, Burros came up with a blintze and told Frankhouser that it was good Jew food he had obtained in a Jew shop. The danger of being unmasked never materialized, but time and again Burros courted the risk.

Only once or twice would Burros let his guard down about his parents. To Frankhouser he once said:

"Boy, this is killing my parents. I wish there was something I could do but I can't. I've got to continue. I know it's for the best someday, but right now they have got to suffer, because the only thing that can logically happen is that they're going to suffer. And they haven't even begun to suffer yet."

Frankhouser told him his parents were "on me, too, but it isn't quite that bad." And Burros said, "Well, if you only knew, Roy, if you only knew."

Chapter Twelve

The American National Party did not get much press attention, but it did fascinate the special antisubversive squad of the police department of New York City.

The squad knew the names of every member of the party, and spot-checks were kept on each. In the late 1950's and early 1960's, more became involved than a simple security watch designed to keep an eye on the "nuts" when important foreigners were in town.

Detectives assigned to the squad came to feel that there was a particular kind of danger in these groups—not to foreign delegates particularly but to the city itself. This is how one of them put it:

"These young toughs live and breathe the atmosphere of violence. That's all they talk about—'getting' this guy or blowing up this or that. A lot of them have guns and it is as if they are making love to them. They are not 'for' anything, but they are against an awful lot of things and people.

"They all got excited, you might say they got aroused, by the civil rights movement. It got them all worked up. They had targets and they worked themselves up more and more, and they found that some people listened to their talk of 'kikes' and 'niggers' and 'spicks' and they loved it more and more. They are 'anti' and we are dealing with the potential of a new kind of crime, the 'anti' crime, hate crime. Most of these people are liars and not smart and most of them are cowards, but they work on each other and we have to watch to make sure that they don't get each other worked up to the point where they have to prove their manhood by going out and killing people."

It is not particularly difficult to keep an eye on the right-fringe. The detectives watch the Yorkville and Queens hang-outs and the bookstores that sell hate literature, check printing companies and mail drops. Burros was part of the world of racist letter-writers and his dossier was thick. Much of the information the squad gets comes directly from the splinter party members themselves. Burros, like most of the other Nazis and pseudo-Nazis, relished his role as informer.

Like Rockwell, Burros enjoyed dealing with the detectives who came to see him. Like Rockwell, he loved the feeling that he was "in" with the police, it gave him a kind of official feeling, it added to the titillation of masquerade and posing.

The information Burros passed on was rarely of much use or news to the police—bits of background about Nazis, details of where meetings were to be held. Burros never gave an inch in his devotion to Nazism and his detestation of the Jews in his talks with the police, but "the Dwarf" loved the idea that he and the police were somehow good guys together.

Burros never took any money for informing but frequently would take the initiative by calling his police contacts. The detectives thought of him as effeminate but more intelligent than most of his friends and comrades, including Rockwell. They knew that he was full of fury and passion at fringe meetings, but with them he was quiet and well-spoken. They noted carefully that he had a way of laughing suddenly and nervously, an uncontrollable cackle and that he seemed to be getting rather more desperate as time went on. (After President Kennedy was assassinated, Burros appeared for a talk with a police contact wearing a button he had had printed: "Lee Harvey Oswald Fan Club.")

The American National Party lasted for just about a year. Burros and Patler had a falling out about the picketing of a racial integration rally in Englewood, New Jersey. Patler was arrested, and sent to jail for ten days. He started a hunger strike in jail and was angry when Burros did not give him enough moral support. Patler also felt that Burros had not shown enough enthusiasm about picketing, and was particularly annoyed at Burros' decision to watch a ball game on TV rather than picket Eleanor Roosevelt's funeral in Poughkeepsie on November 19, 1962. Patler and a friend did picket, and Patler carried a sign, "Ship her smelly corpse back to Moscow." He was arrested and sentenced to ninety days. When he was released—on a habeas corpus filed by the American Civil Liberties Union—he decided he had had enough of Burros and that Rockwell was his leader after all. When he told his wife that he was returning to Rockwell, she decided she had had enough and they were divorced. Patler again became a Rockwell lieutenant.

For a while, Burros was without a leader or a club. But he kept busy and seemed happy. He had money for steaks in the Yorkville restaurants, there was a street fight he could get into now and then and talk about for weeks afterward, there were the *Wehrmacht* veterans. He had a little following and they would laugh at his jokes and chuckle about his Jew-killing machines. He had his correspondence, with racists in the United States and Britain and South Africa and West Germany. Sometimes he would make street-corner speeches. Dan and his friends often did that, less to be heard than to prove a point to themselves. He would say that he had to go up to Yorkville to make a speech, to "draw a line" for himself to cross over.

"If I don't go when I draw a line," he once said, "there would be another line and the next one and I would be crawling inside myself."

There were books to read—memoirs of German generals, stories of World War II battles, books by survivors of concentration camps to be annotated for discrepancies. And special books. *Mein Kampf,* to be read and reread so that Burros could astonish and delight his audiences at the Yorkville bars with his memorized quotations. There was Nietzsche from whom to extract sentences about strength and power and the weakness of love and women. There was Spengler's *Decline of the West.* And from one of his literary sources Burros drew the Latin translation of the Greek axiom: *Docunt volenten fata nolentem trahunt*—The fates lead the one who is unwilling. (Later Burros was to use this axiom, slightly misquoting it, as the motto of *The Free American,* a violently racist and aggressive Nazi newssheet that became much admired among the fascist cognoscenti in this country and abroad.)

Burros did not read much fiction, but he did treasure a paperback sex-and-action thriller called *The Grave of Heroes,* about a Latin American dictatorship. He said he was just like one of the characters in the book—a pudgy, murderous security chief who had men knifed and tortured, the silent, powerful, feared man behind the dictator, El Jefe. Almost every passage of violent sex and painful death was underlined by Burros.

Perhaps most of all, Burros admired a book called *Imperium,* printed in the United States in 1962, two years after the death of its author, Francis Parker Yockey.

Yockey was born in Chicago in 1917. He was graduated

cum laude from Notre Dame and went on to get a law degree there in 1938. During World War II he served briefly in the Army, got a medical discharge, became assistant county attorney of Warren County in Michigan, and then was appointed to the legal staff prosecuting "second-string" Nazis at the war crimes trials in Wiesbaden in 1946. He had resigned after eleven months, charging that the evidence was doctored to convict the Nazis and serve the purposes of Communism.

Imperium is an attempt to develop a "logical, historical" rationale for racism and authoritarianism and rule by the West. The book is anti-Semitic, but Yockey develops a theory that Jews are defined by attitude and philosophy not by birth alone and that the last act of life, the moment of death, is all-important. He writes:

> Thus, in Western life, we are not unfamiliar with the man who, after associating with Jews, reading their literature, and adopting their viewpoint, actually becomes a Jew in the fullest sense of the word. It is not necessary that he have "Jewish blood." The converse is also known. Many Jews have adopted Western feelings and thereby acquired Western race.

About life and death:

> An age of action lives side by side with death and values life by its attitude toward death. The old Goth religious idea is still with us—it is in his last moment that a man shows what is in him in its purity. Though he may have been a wastrel, he may die a hero and it is this last act of his life that will survive in the minds of his descendants. We cannot possibly value a life according to its length, as materialism did or believe in any doctrine of immortality of the body.

In June, 1960, Yockey was arrested in San Francisco for fraudulently holding three passports. He committed suicide in the city jail on June 17, 1960, by swallowing potassium cyanide.

Burros read Yockey over and over, talked about *Imperium* with his friends. He had little to say about Yockey's idea that a Jew could cleanse himself of Jewishness. In Yorkville, Burros was still known admiringly as the man who wanted to kill all the Jews, every one. But he did talk about the moment of death, the moment of truth, and how it meant more than a whole lifetime.

But without a party, without a club, without a leader, and without uniforms, Burros felt lost and rudderless and sometimes used to say so to his friends in Yorkville. He attended meetings of a half-dozen splinter groups and then selected one to join—the National Renaissance Party.

Although the NRP was not much bigger than the other fringe clubs—about twenty or thirty members—and had almost no reputation outside the fringes, Burros found it *gemütlich*. For one thing, the party had been in existence for years and that made it practically a historical institution. For another, its founder and leader, James H. Madole, was, like Rockwell, an "older" man—he was thirty-seven—who could be looked up to (but at the same time he had the virtue of hating Rockwell). The party supplied its members with uniforms. It had a permanent headquarters in Madole's Manhattan apartment at 10 West 90th Street. And—for Burros possibly the strongest appeal of all—the leader had a mother who lived with him, a mother who heartily endorsed her son's activities. Mrs. Madole, a tall, gray-haired woman, embodied all the forceful Germanic qualities that Burros adored; she was as rabidly and outspokenly anti-Semitic as her son.

Burros was not much impressed with Madole's personality.

Madole was a thin, anemic man who suffered from chronic asthma, and he could not stand excitement. Burros was irritated by his glibness and found him "mouthy."

Burros had been in touch with Madole even before he joined Rockwell. He had written to Madole on a piece of parchment paper decorated with a swastika—as part of his hobby of making pen pals among the right-extremists. After the American National Party disintegrated in the feud with Patler, Burros attended a few NRP meetings in Yorkville, and one day in the spring of 1963 signed up—on condition that he could be a member of Madole's "Security Echelon" —the little band of toughs who got to wear the uniforms of black and gold.

If Burros was a bit contemptuous of Madole, Madole, in turn, was always just a little bit nervous about Burros. There was the habit Burros had of saying things in public that might better be said in private, in the family—like extermination of the Jews or dropping nuclear bombs and germ bombs on China. Madole thought the latter particularly might be rather impractical because the germs, not knowing they were anti-Communist, might travel on the wind to other countries.

The swastika fetish upset Madole a trifle, too, particularly when Burros wanted to paint swastikas on Madole's own lamps; Madole used to say that if he would let him, Burros would put swastikas on Madole's underwear. And since Madole regarded Rockwell as his competitor for attention and leadership—a compliment Rockwell did not seem to reciprocate—he was always watching for Rockwell spies in his midst; he thought it possible that Burros might be such a spy.

Madole and some of his boys liked to think of themselves as rather more sophisticated in their racism than the Rockwell band—only certain key Jews were worth bothering to vilify—and Burros' enthusiasm about killing every last Jew was sometimes faintly embarrassing.

But Burros was in some ways an asset to the party; he was well known as a veteran of racist and Nazi organizations; his collection of Nazi souvenirs had given him some celebrity.

It was at a NRP get-together that Burros first met Frank Rotella, an employee for the New York City Department of Welfare, an enthusiastic racist. Burros was modeling his uniform for a group that included a few men who said they were former officers of the German Army. The uniform bore a thunderbolt emblem, and Burros and the Germans noted carefully that it was similar to the insignia of the Nazi SS, a thought that delighted Burros enormously.

At another meeting, Burros showed Rotella one of the prizes of his collection—a pre-World War II book in German showing "atrocities" committed by Poles against Germans. Burros relished the gruesome pictures, but Rotella found them just a bit distasteful and said so.

Burros was furious, claimed that Rotella had insulted Hitler's honor, and demanded an apology. Rotella declined laughingly and Burros said he was talking just like a Jew. (Rotella became scornful of Madole; he said Madole was in the NRP just for the money he could collect and that he was not a hard enough worker. Rotella wandered off into the Ku Klux Klan, was dismissed from his job in the Department of Welfare. But he kept in touch with Burros; they would help each other put out little leaflets and brochures.)

The National Renaissance Party never had quite the appeal for Burros that the American Nazi Party had; after a while it began to seem second-rate. Annoyed by Madole's nervousness about swastikas, Burros sometimes used to speak wistfully of the good old days in the Arlington barracks where a Nazi came right out and said he was a Nazi. Once in a while, one or another of Rockwell's troopers would come to the city and get in touch with Burros, who always responded eagerly and gratefully.

Burros felt a listlessness in himself those days. He used to say he was not getting anywhere, that Madole was just a bag of wind, that the Jews were getting stronger and stronger, that he needed action. He enrolled for karate lessons, determined, this time, to master the art. He talked about how when the day came he would kill Jews with his own hands. He went around looking for fist fights and found one in the Bronx one day.

Some Italian-Americans were giving a party and Burros and some of his friends were invited. Burros turned the conversation to the glory and infallibility of Hitler, there were some words and Burros invited one of the guests out to fight. The battle lasted ten or fifteen minutes and both men were bloodied. Bystanders pulled them apart, Burros shouting that he would fight to the death to defend Hitler's honor.

Although Burros was contemptuous of the NRP, it did bring him his first taste of martyrdom behind bars. In July of 1963, New York rarely used the word "summer" without preceding it with "long, hot." The cliché became the summation of all the fears of New York that the civil rights drive, shifted from the South to the streets of northern cities and gathering momentum, could lead to riots and bloodshed.

As the police had feared, trouble was building not only from the civil rights movement and the pent-up fury of Negroes who felt that their moment had to come now or never, but from northern racists excited by the scent of action and blood. Men like Rockwell and Madole and their underlings felt that their moment was at hand, too, that the anger and fear and resentment of whites would give the racists what they had always lacked—acceptance and identity. Throughout the feverish city, the little bands of Nazis and racists met to plan counter-picketing demonstrations against the civil rights groups.

The clear goal was provocation. The civil rights picketers carried signs demanding jobs; the counter-marchers carried signs mocking "niggers" and "coons."

One of the targets of the Congress for Racial Equality (CORE) was the chain of White Castle diners whose hiring policy, the civil rights group claimed, discriminated against Negroes. Tension centered around the White Castle Diner at Soundview Avenue and Bruckner Boulevard in the Bronx, where neighborhood toughs lined up to jeer the CORE marchers.

On the night of July 13, 1963, there was a meeting at Madole's house to plan a counter-demonstration at the White Castle. Madole was there, his mother, Burros, and four other men: party member Edward Cassidy, nineteen, known at headquarters as "Madole's faithful little dog" and, like Burros, a major in the Security Echelon; twenty-one-year-old John Corrigan, twenty-six-year-old Peter Krauss, and thirty-six-year-old Paul Joachim, none of them official members of the NRP, all of them free-lance sympathizers with its aims. The group met to prepare racist leaflets to distribute at the diner.

Later that night, Cassidy, Corrigan, Krauss, and Joachim left Madole's house and drove in a truck to the neighborhood of the diner. Their plan was to shout insults at the CORE picketers and in case of physical counterattack to fall back to the truck for protection and weapons.

At Bruckner Boulevard they were joined by twenty-six-year-old Anthony Wells, a former member of Rockwell's group, and twenty-two-year-old Ian Lehr, an ex-member of a defunct rightist group called the Fighting American Nationalists.

In the diner, Joachim flung the leaflets prepared at Madole's house into the ranks of the picketing CORE members. "This will let you know we are not with you," he shouted. When that got no reply, another member of the group yelled, "Let's get out of here, it smells like a zoo," and another jeered, "What do you expect when there's nothing but niggers?"

That brought a response. One enraged CORE picketer began wrestling with Joachim. Police, who had been keeping an eye on the picketers, broke up the fight and Madole's band retreated to their truck, where they were surrounded by a crowd of furious Negroes. With police help, they managed to drive free. Joachim, Cassidy, and Corrigan dropped Wells, Lehr, and Krauss at a subway station and then drove to the 43rd Precinct police station. By this time it was 4 A.M. of July 14.

Leaving Corrigan in the truck, Joachim and Cassidy entered the police station and told the desk officer they wanted to make a complaint. They were referred to Detective William Rooney, who remembered seeing both of them at the diner. They told Detective Rooney that they had been assaulted by CORE members and that their truck had been damaged.

Detective Rooney went out to inspect the truck, in which Corrigan was still waiting, and found a bit more than the complainants had wanted to exhibit. He found racist leaflets and an attaché case. Inside the case were a fully loaded .22 caliber revolver and more racist leaflets. Also in the truck was a pellet gun with a box of pellets, loaded tear-gas weapons, a crossbow loaded with a steel-tipped arrow, a butcher knife, a switchblade knife, a straight razor, two masks, a long-handled ax, and two gun holsters.

The police arrested Corrigan, Joachim, and Cassidy and—after Cassidy had obligingly supplied their home addresses—rounded up Krauss, Lehr, and Wells.

Later that day, Burros appeared at Madole's house in a state of great agitation. He had just heard a radio news bulletin. "All our fellows have been arrested," he cried. Before Madole had a chance to turn on the radio to confirm the news, police in civilian clothes knocked on the door and arrested them both—although Burros, when questioned, said he had no part in the attack on the CORE members, knew nothing about any planned violence by the NRP. He had been busy stapling literature together during the meeting, he said, and had paid no attention to the discussion.

All the defendants were indicted, accused of conspiring and creating a disturbance and breach of public peace by circulating inflammatory literature and of being armed with firearms, knives, and a crossbow. They were released on bail.

It took ten months for the case to inch its way up the crowded calendar of the court. During that year, Burros continued to correspond with racists throughout the world and attend meetings of the NRP. He worked as a printer in the city and for a few months at the Olympic Machine & Tool Company, in Tillson, New York. Burros got room and board and a few dollars spending money. He spent most of his time in his room, writing anti-Semitic pamphlets.

The trial opened on May 4, 1964, before Judge Irwin T. Davidson. Madole, Burros, Cassidy, and Krauss shared a lawyer—a rightist attorney named John D. Graves. The others had individual lawyers.

Madole indignantly denied that he had sent his men into trouble where he would not go himself.

Burros, on the stand, dodged the question for a while as to whether he had suspected there would be trouble. When Judge Davidson reminded him he had told detectives that he thought there would be trouble, Burros finally admitted, "Well, I suspected there would be trouble at the Bronx, your Honor."

The trial droned on without much excitement, but reporters present sat up straight and began to take notes when Detective Thomas Martino took the stand to testify about picking up Ian Lehr at his home. Detective Martino testified that in the apartment he saw a Jewish calendar. In the car riding to the police station, Martino said, he asked Lehr if he were Jewish and the answer was yes.

Martino, over the objections of Lehr's attorney, Perez Rosenthal, testified that Lehr had told him he did not belong to the NRP but did belong to the American Nazi Party.

"I asked him at that time, I said: If you are Jewish, how can you belong to an organization like this? He said, Well, the members don't know that I am Jewish.

"Well, I said, do you know what they stand for? He said: Yes. I said: The annihilation of the Jews and other minority groups. He said: That's right. I said: Do you still belong to it? He said: Yes, you see I am a coward. I belong to nothing and I have accomplished nothing in my life and I belong to this just to belong and to be able to do something. He said: Now I feel like somebody when I belong to this group."

During this testimony, Burros stared impassively at Lehr. Occasionally he doodled but kept staring. All through the trial, except for this bit of testimony, Burros looked curiously around the courtroom and seemed to be enjoying himself. Several people noticed him particularly, because he seemed to have such a swagger when he walked, seemed so full of confidence and exuberance.

There was another Burros who sat in the Bronx courtroom during the trial. His name was Robert Burros and, although he had not participated in the White Castle Diner fracas, he was a devoted member of the National Renaissance Party, and greatly interested in the fate of his fellow-members. Born in 1937, Robert Burros was a native of Newburgh, New York. He and Daniel Burros used to talk about the fact that they had the same name, and explored the possibility that they might be related. But neither explored it very thoroughly—Daniel because, of course, he was concealing his parents' Jewishness, and Robert because he too had something to conceal.

Later, after the name Burros was in headlines across the country, Robert Burros admitted his own father was Jewish. He was criticized at first by the NRP for having concealed this interesting fact, but his credentials as a devout racist and faithful servitor of Madole were accepted, and he was allowed to continue to serve. As a matter of fact, he became something of a drawing card and publicity getter—the "Jew boy" who saw the light.

Robert Burros was a tense man with a compulsion to talk. He was bar-mitzvahed but, he has said, it was against his will; his mother was a "pure-blooded Aryan" and he was not biologically a Jew.

"My father was Jewish, but he saw the viewpoint of the National Renaissance Party," he once told an interviewer. "My father was an American patriot, my father always advocated America first, and my father saw that what Zionism was doing to this country was ruinous and was disastrous. My father believed in the supremacy of the white race, my father always spoke in favor of the supremacy of the white race. . . . My father always ridiculed the Jews . . . you see, the Jews . . . he's always preaching that the Jews must control the world and the Jews are so fanatical in this dedication that in order to control the world they are willing to see the rest of the world destroyed so that they can control it. That's how fanatical and paranoid the Jewish nation is. Now my father always opposed this. My father was always an American first. . . .

"I found the Jewish language and the Jewish culture so alien to me that I just could not assimilate the culture, the religion, the philosophy into my intellectual bloodstream."

The jury went out at 3 P.M. on June 9. It returned at 4:55 P.M. the next day. All the defendants except Corrigan were found guilty of conspiracy. All except Corrigan and Lehr were found guilty of riot. Corrigan and Lehr were found guilty of unlawful assembly. Burros, Madole, Cassidy, and Joachim were found guilty of possessing firearms. All except Burros, Corrigan, and Lehr were found guilty of possessing dangerous instruments with the intent to use them against others.

Lehr's attorney made an emotional plea for his client: "Somewhere along the line something went wrong."

The judge sentenced Madole to one to two years in state prison, the maximum sentence for incitement to riot without participation in the riot. The same sentence was handed down for Burros.

In passing sentence, the judge said:

"Not the least regrettable aspect of this whole incident is

the fact that the defendants Madole and Burros—the more sophisticated members of the group—did not hesitate to recruit for their malevolent purposes young men whom they succeeded in injecting with their own virus of hate."

In the case of Lehr, convicted of three misdemeanors, the Court said the defendant was entitled to sympathy: "He is a confused, inadequate, insecure individual" and confinement would destroy the possibility of rehabilitating him to normal life." The Court suspended sentence on Lehr and placed him on probation for three years.

On July 24, 1964, Burros, Madole, and Anthony Wells were sent to Sing Sing, the state penitentiary at Ossining. (The other convicted men were sent to other prisons.) They were assigned to a reception company that included about one hundred and fifty other recent arrivals and placed, in accordance with the prison custom, in a segregated area for fourteen days of orientation, lectures, physical examinations, psychological, educational achievement and aptitude tests.

Burros occupied a cell six by nine feet between Madole and Wells. He seemed quite content in his quarters—the cell was furnished with a steel-frame bed, writing stand, chair, toilet, and sink—and his gusto for the prison food astonished his fellow-inmates. He was neither repentant nor resentful at being locked up but, rather, seemed to look on his sentence as a kind of martyrdom to be endured for the sake of his principles. He played checkers with Madole and beat him; he sought and found the equivalent of street-corner audiences during recreation periods and made something of a prison reputation with his anti-Semitic comments about other prisoners, particularly some of the Jewish trusties. "There's the guy who wants to make lampshades out of us," the prisoners would jeer.

Burros might have grown sulky if the martyrdom had been protracted. But he did not stay in Sing Sing even long enough to complete the two-week orientation period. He was released ten days after his arrival—on August 4—on a certificate of reasonable doubt (his case was being appealed) and Madole was released about a week later. Burros' release was securied when bail of $7,500 was posted by his uncle, a brother of Esther Burros.

Chapter Thirteen

There was an emptiness, a flatness, an almost unbearable sense of futility in Burros' life after the White Castle trial and Sing Sing, and for a long while he did not know why.

There was certainly plenty for him to do. He was making a name for himself in the fringe world, not only in the United States but among British and German and Australian and French fascists, who read his little newspaper—*The International Nazi Fascist* it was called sometimes and the *Nazi Fascist* at others—and sent him cautiously admiring letters.

He replied to one such letter three days after he left Sing Sing. The tone of the letter was subdued but proud, as befitted a newly made martyr, and began, "As you know I was imprisoned." The letter conveyed, also, the old aura of secrecy and defiance. ("I had the papers hidden in case my friends the police decided to confiscate. It is too much trouble getting out a newspaper to have it destroyed by a bunch of stupid cops.")

It would have pleased Burros to know that his name was filed in the dossiers of the German and British police and that some of his broadsheets ("There's Nothing Wrong with America that a Pogrom Wouldn't Cure"—the headline in German type) were distributed at neo-Nazi meetings in West Germany.

There were letters to write to members of Rockwell's band who had split away and were working for the cause on their own, letters to write and newspapers to trade. Sometimes he would even see current members of the Rockwell gang and despite his apostasy they would clap each other on the back. Often Burros talked of returning to Rockwell, but it never came to anything. Madole was beginning to fall in Burros' eyes; he seemed to be nothing more than a windbag, and Rockwell shone by comparison—and in retrospect.

Madole and Burros finally parted company because, Madole later said, Burros was still too fond of Rockwell. Burros did not miss the National Renaissance Party. He had decided it was just more talk, talk, talk. He still had the *Wehrmacht* veterans in Yorkville, still could show up as a kind of unaffiliated picket at left-wing and liberal activities. And, to fill in time, he wrote about and studied Odinism, the "religion of the Viking gods." He never got very deeply into it but relished Odinism's rejection of the weakling Christ.

But somehow, somehow nothing seemed to have any salt anymore. In Yorkville one night Burros toyed with his soft drink at a table wet with beer. For a while, the talk was about Jew-killing and Burros seemed his old self, eyes glistening, palms sweating, voice rising. But he slipped back quickly into moroseness, was silent while the talk went on around him. He left, walked the streets, popped in and out of a few of his favorite bars, came back, sat down heavily. There was a pause, and Burros said, "Where are we getting, where are we getting? The same people all the time. We are not reaching anybody!"

More and more often, he talked about not being able to break out, of being isolated. He developed a theory—a man feels he wants to do something and feels he can't do it alone. He joins other people who feel the same way but they can't break out and reach people, so he is alone with them and it is the same as being alone by himself, only the mathematics are different. "You have to have a current," he would say, "you have to be part of electricity or you are alone."

It became an obsession. The leadership principle was correct, he would say, but the leader could not exist alone; he had to have a base, people to reach. A Hitler, a god like Hitler, could create his own base, but in America there were no Hitlers yet. What was needed, what Burros needed and wanted, was to be part of a meaningfully large group of people awaiting the leader. In Yorkville he used to say that at least the damned Jews were waiting for their Messiah *together* and you couldn't take that away from them.

In 1965, Burros found what he was looking for, an organization with roots—people, a group with real people all over the country, not just letterheads. He found it through a combination of a scratchy old movie, a one-eyed racist from Pennsylvania, and a meeting in Bear, Delaware.

The movie was "Birth of a Nation," made in 1915 from the book *The Clansman* and referred to by the Klan as part of its recruiting drive. Burros saw it in a revival at the Museum of Modern Art and afterward he talked about it endlessly. It was just like the beginning of the Nazi movement, he said, the same ideas, real organization. But he decided gloomily that something had happened to the Ku Klux Klan, that it had gone dead.

Roy Frankhouser changed his mind. Frankhouser was a short, lean, neat, dark-haired man with a wide smile. He had lost his left eye in a barroom brawl; the glass eye he wore, the intensity of his speech—he had a habit of interjecting sound effects into his sentences—and his flamboyant gestures gave him a somewhat theatrical flavor.

Frankhouser and Burros had resumed their acquaintance after Burros left Rockwell. Burros admired Frankhouser's facility at public speaking and Frankhouser was convinced that Burros was what the Klan needed—an intellectual racist. The two men would meet in New York whenever Frankhouser had enough money saved to come in from Reading, Pennsylvania.

They would walk the streets, wander Yorkville, drop in at steakhouses (Frankhouser would watch in stunned astonishment while Burros devoured two steaks at a sitting). Sometimes Burros would leave Frankhouser to go off and see a prostitute he frequented, a brassy looking woman called Molly.

Some of Burros' friends used to tell him she looked like a Jew girl, but he always denied it. Mostly, Burros and Frankhouser would talk about the need to save white America, about the Klan and the need for a "grass roots" organization to fight the Jews and Negroes.

The Klan was avid for devoted "leaders" in the North. The "realms"—state organizations—in New York and New Jersey and Pennsylvania had only about fifty members each and northerners like Frankhouser were cherished and promoted, almost as soon as they signed up, to "Grand Dragons" —state chairmen—if they showed any signs of being willing to devote their time to the Klan.

On July 28, 1965, Frankhouser invited Burros to accompany him to a Klan meeting in Bear, Delaware.

Burros had never attended a meeting like that. He lived in a world where ten or fifteen people got together for cell meetings, a world of shouting at street corners to attract passersby, of feeding off the crowds gathered by the enemy. He looked around the field at Bear and saw crowds of men and women who were like him in their hatred of Jews and

Negroes; thousands of people, 13,000 by Frankhouser's account.

Burros grabbed Frankhouser, and said, "This is it! This is the way to capture the American imagination! Mass movement. This is the reality of the mass movement."

Yes, Frankhouser agreed, the Klan was the answer. But suddenly Burros was dejected.

"I can't join them," he told Frankhouser.

"Why?"

"Well, you know, the code and everything."

What Burros explained—and what Frankhouser listened to with complete seriousness—was that Burros, as an Odinist who did not believe in Christ but in the war gods of the Norse people, could not fulfill the Klan's membership requirement of faith in Christianity.

Frankhouser insisted there was a way out.

"Do you like Christ and everything?"

Burros thought that over.

"Yes, I dig him and everything," he said. "I understand him. I understand the Christian idea and I'm with it. I'm still with the Christian West."

Frankhouser said:

"Well, I think God and the Klan would understand this. You can join and I'll swear by you."

Frankhouser approached Robert M. Shelton, the Imperial Wizard, and told him about Burros. There was bad blood between Rockwell and the KKK, and Shelton had rejected other members of the American Nazi Party, but he decided to make an exception for Burros, as he had quit Rockwell.

"Roy, will you swear by this man?" Shelton asked.

"I'll swear by Dan Burros as I would my own life," Frankhouser said. "This man is one hundred percent."

"I'm going in on this with my life," Burros declared, when

he learned the Klan would accept him. "I'll do my best, Mr. Shelton. If you let me in, I'll fight until I'm dead."

Burros joined the Klan that day, and entered the happiest period of his life.

First, there was a richness of uniforms. There was the regulation white gown and hood that he got when he joined. At meetings in the South he would sometimes wear the uniform of the Klan security guard—black boots, belt, flashlight for direction of traffic. Occasionally he would give little speeches in the South at Klan meetings, worded as simply as possible "not to go over their heads," mostly about how the North stood with the South and they were in this fight against mongrelization together.

And almost immediately Burros became Grand Dragon of New York and had a distinctive uniform to wear—the scarlet gown befitting his rank. Burros was promoted for two reasons—there were not many hard workers to choose from, and Frankhouser and others believed that what the Klan needed was an "intellectual" patina from people like Burros.

A Klan leader said once to Burros, "You got some good points. Now you put that on paper and bring it in and we're going to try to work on it. We're going to have to put more men on it because we're not used to this. We're country folk around here and we can still use your ideas." Flattered beyond anything he had experienced before, Burros embraced Shelton as his new leader—"Here's a man I can follow."

Burros became Grand Dragon; he was also King Kleagle —organizer for New York State.

He was in charge of two rival Klaverns and became adept at bridging the hatred between them. The "uptown" Klavern held its meetings in a fourth floor apartment at 1762 First Avenue in Yorkville. Twenty to thirty people would show up for a meeting. Newcomers were welcomed—but cautiously; they might be undercover agents. Burros followed the prescribed procedure for inviting potential members to his meetings. When a letter from a would-be joiner in his area was passed on to him, usually by the National Office of the United Klans of America, Burros would send this reply:

> We thank you for your interest in the organization. Every Saturday (unless the Security Guard Attachment is on a mission) we hold a Klavern meeting . . . [here Burros gave the Yorkville address]. When you knock on the door give the password "Action Now." This is only a temporary password for applicants; this is NOT the KKK password. You will only receive the KKK password after you have been investigated, qualified for membership, and received the oath.

Burros would open each meeting by asking, "Has anybody got any problems?" The purpose was to create a sense of solidarity, of one for all. Sometimes a Klan member would say he was broke and Burros would arrange for a small loan. A Klan member might be out of a job and another would recommend him to his boss. The rest of the meeting was mostly indoctrination—speeches by Burros and other members, denunciations of Jews and Negroes, readings from the collected works of Robert Shelton or other Klan leaders. Oaths were exchanged, passwords arranged, and that was about all. Burros ran a tightly disciplined meeting and was admired on First Avenue.

He was also admired "downtown." The downtown Klavern was made up of a different kind of membership than the clerks and other office workers who attended the First Avenue meetings. Downtown were men from the docks, who sometimes showed up with their bale hooks slung over their shoulders, tautly eager for action, not talk or oaths. "Let's get the niggers," somebody would shout. Burros would say he wanted to get the niggers as much as anybody else but, "Look, boys, you have to use your head." He would tell them how action has to be planned, how they were in something big, how they had to get around the cops, how they had to have discipline to prepare for the day that would come.

Downtown they cursed the uptown Klavern, called it the "Panty Klan." But they respected Burros and listened to him because he would tell them he knew how it was with them, that he knew what it was like living in a rat trap, being caught and wanting to break out. Sometimes he lived with the downtown boys and they liked him.

"I've got to keep those two Klaverns apart or the downtown Klan will rip them up," he would tell Frankhouser. "The guys from the waterfront will murder them."

Burros recruited a few members—and rejected at least one applicant. A letter came to him one day from a man with a distinctly Jewish name who wanted to enlist in the fight against Negroes.

Burros replied, a handwritten letter under the letterhead Knights of the Ku Klux Klan, Realm of New York, United Klans of America, bearing his mail drop address, 152 West 42 Street, Suite 536:

> Thank you for your interest in the Ku Klux Klan. We have a unit here in New York. We can give you an address where you can meet us or we can come visit you.
>
> I have a question. I hope you will not feel insulted but your name sounds very Jewish. I realize it could also be Polish or German. Write me and let me know if you are a Christian. Jews are not eligible to join the Klan. Also, do not lie be-

cause we have ways of checking. Right now our investigators are pretty busy and we would not want to embarrass you if you are Jewish.

The applicant wrote again, demanding to know why Jews were excluded. This time Burros' answer was typewritten:

> The reasons we exclude persons of Jewish faith is that Jesus Christ is lauded at every KKK meeting and all meetings are opened and closed with Christian prayer. We would not like to get Jewish members because of patriotism and then have them leave offended because of our rites.

Burros and Frankhouser grew closer. They would meet at Frankhouser's home in Reading and talk tactics and listen to music; Burros preferred Wagner.

Frankhouser talked a lot about his family and how he came to be a KKK man and a racist. He talked about how, when he was eight years old, his father told him not to play with Negroes and how his father warned him that "niggers" were different, not like everybody else. Frankhouser's father, who was a musician then, eventually joined the Klan and bitterness grew in the family. There was a divorce and Frankhouser lived in a children's home for a while.

"Living in a children's home," he once said, "I admired strength. I lived in a society that seemed to be absolutely weak. They could break up my family and throw me into a home and where was the all-American bounty? What kind of country was this?"

Burros almost never talked about his family with Frankhouser. Some of the racists who got into arguments with Burros used to whisper that he was a Jew or a Jew agent—standard feud procedure within the fringe, but Frankhouser used to laugh because nobody was more anti-Semitic than Burros.

In Reading once, Frankhouser visited his mother with Burros. There was a photograph of a young boy—the son of a friend of Frankhouser's mother, taken at his bar mitzvah, with skullcap and prayer shawl.

Burros looked at it in amazement and said to Frankhouser: "Is that you?"

Frankhouser was petrified. He knew that if the mere idea of his being Jewish got around he would be "shot or something, thrown out of all the organizations."

"No, my goodness, Dan, absolutely not." Frankhouser jumped up, kept denying that the picture was of him, and while he shouted, knew that Burros might think he was protesting too much, making too much of it. On the way back from Frankhouser's house, Burros suddenly said:

"Are you sure you're not really Jewish? You can tell me."

"No, I'm not Jewish. I mean that's just a friend of mine. I get along with some Jews. Maybe you can't, but I can."

Burros shook his head, smiled.

"You are Jewish."

"No, no, man, I'm not."

Burros let it go at that. The only things he said about his parents was about his father's war record and that Frankhouser should not talk much over the phone if he called Burros' home.

"If you talk to my mother give her the minimum of information and she will give it to me and I'll call you right away. My mother's scared to death of my activities and it'll create dissension in the house."

Frankhouser thought this entirely understandable because most of his comrades had family trouble growing out of their activities. Occasionally he would accompany Burros to within a block or two of his parents' home in Queens and he took the neighborhood for Jewish. He thought Burros was brave, taking chances living in a Jewish neighborhood.

(Burros told two sets of stories about his parents' reaction to his Klan and Nazi activities. To some friends he said that they had better steer clear of his parents because they might reveal information. To others he boasted that he had his mother "scared to death" with warnings that he "would take care of them" if they talked.)

Once in the South, staying at a motel for a Klan meeting, Frankhouser and Burros were joined by a German who had been in the Hitler Youth. Frankhouser was tired and said, "Boy, you two are really master-racers; I can't keep up with you." Frankhouser made some remark about how blond and blue-eyed the two others were and said jokingly that his own dark looks would have put him in the gas chamber in Nazi Germany.

"Oh, no, Roy," said Burros. "If you only knew."

These occasional near-lapses by Burros, these quickly conquered impulses to let the mask slip an inch so he could be seen, sometimes raised fleeting doubts in Frankhouser's mind. But they vanished immediately because of Burros' devotion to the racist cause, because nobody Frankhouser knew was more immediately and passionately devoted to making the Jews pay.

Frankhouser and Burros agreed that the Jews were making a good thing "propagandizing" about the gas chambers but sometimes, just for argument's sake, Frankhouser would say something to the Jews' "credit," in connection with the Arabs, for instance. Burros always defended the Arabs, but Frankhouser thought they were "worse than niggers."

"With the Jews you have a culture and a civilization. . . . To some degree the Jews represent Western civilization, but by trying to identify themselves with the emerging African nations this was going to be the Jews' downfall."

Burros wouldn't listen and he wouldn't listen to any of Frankhouser's rationalizations that the gas chambers were a fabrication to keep Jews loyal to Zionism.

"Well," Burros said one day, "I can tell you for a fact that there is some truth to it. But it was justifiable. Germany was fighting for her life. They couldn't feed the population in the cities. How could they feed a population within a population?"

Sometimes Frankhouser would wonder if the Jews perhaps couldn't be cured of their "anti-Gentilism" and that would rouse Burros:

"No, they've got to suffer and suffer. They've got to see it this way or be totally annihilated. You've got to bring them to see that unless they change and adapt to Western civilization they will be destroyed."

Sometimes they would argue about Christianity and Jesus Christ. Burros would say that despite his Klan oath to Jesus Christ he was still an Odinist.

"What in heck is an Odinist?" Frankhouser demanded one day. "Is it something like Wotan, Brunhilde or stuff like that? Do you really believe in the myths of the ancient forest and the gods of the forest and of death?"

"Yes, I do," said Burros. "I don't see much use for religion, period. But people must have it to keep them within bounds. The Commandments are good, the Lord's Prayer. These are things we can build civilization on. A heritage, we can't throw it out the window."

But as for Jesus Christ, Burros said he was not for him:

"Personally, I sort of like a guy who has a dramatic outlook on life, war, and death. Philosophy—a clear-cut sword that you can pray to, or slash across your enemy's face. My cross is the hilt of my sword."

For the sake of the Klan, under Frankhouser's persuasion, Burros put aside for a while his obsession with the swastika and agreed not to print it on material he wrote for the Klan.

"Roy," he would say, "if we are going to work with the Klan, we don't want the Klan getting smeared with the Nazis," and Frankhouser would praise him for his acumen and sacrifice.

Frankhouser and Burros seesawed between exultation and weariness. Sometimes Burros would criticize Frankhouser for taking time off from the cause to go to the movies. Other times Burros would say he was exhausted and needed to visit his prostitute friend, Molly. Then he would say he was going to get back into Sing Sing somehow and organize the Negroes into Nazi cells, that he was going to fight and fight and suffer and suffer and nothing could stop him now.

Only once did Frankhouser and Burros get into a spat, and the issue was what Burros took to be his friend's apathy. Frankhouser had finished a speech and point-blank refused to do any more work that day.

"Look, you Aryan, take off, man; I'm bushed. I'm really flipped and I can't go out. I'm done."

Burros was furious.

"Roy, you've got to get off your lazy ass and get out there, you've got to do this."

"Look, don't tell me to get off my lazy ass. I've fought for years in this battle and if you don't like it, you just go to to hell."

Burros turned red, shouted, "Nobody talks to me like that," and began beating the wall with his fist and slamming his body against the wall.

"What the hell are you doing that for?" Frankhouser demanded.

"If I don't do it there, I would do it to you and that I don't want to do."

Frankhouser thought that Burros was going mad, grabbed an automatic and pointed it at him.

"Dan," he shouted, "if you start cracking at me like that I'm going to let one fly at your leg."

Burros kept hammering the wall, shouting that nobody could talk to him like that. He quieted eventually, turned to Frankhouser and said:

"Roy, don't ever do that. I'll never take that from anybody. I'll never take it from anybody that talks to me like that. Roy, if it was anybody else besides you, I would have tried to kill you."

But that was just about the only real fight between Frankhouser and Burros. Burros felt that he had outgrown the bickering and feuding of the Rockwell barracks and used to look back on the Arlington days as a kind of kindergarten, a prelude to the real thing that was the Klan. He had friends, he had a cause, he had rank, and for the first time all three were combined into one organization. And for the first time also—at twenty-eight—he fell in love.

Carol was twenty-four when Burros met her in Yorkville during a German-American Steuben Day parade in the fall of 1965. She was not an unattractive young woman—five feet four, a bit chunky, but well groomed. She had brown eyes, a straight nose, and wore her brown hair in a feathery cut that fell low over her forehead. She used pale pink lipstick on a mouth that was somewhat too full and when she smiled she showed teeth that were a bit crooked. Her speech held the nasal twang of her native Brooklyn, although her grammar was faultless.

According to her own account of her life up to the time she met Burros (and like most members of the fringe movement, she was inclined to be evasive about certain details of personal history), she was the only child of comfortably well-off parents, had attended Hofstra College for two years, was working as a secretary and lived with her family in Long Island. She had been attracted to the racist idea as a young girl, through her father's pro-Southern attitude about the Civil War—"But I only had an academic interest in the whole thing." Several months before meeting Burros she had impulsively attended a White Citizens Council meeting not far from her home in Long Island, where she had met Madole and John Ryan. The atmosphere of racism had proved highly congenial.

It was John Ryan who introduced Carol to Burros after the Steuben Day parade. The three of them, together with half a dozen other young men and women, went to a Yorkville bar to talk over the parade. Burros sat beside Carol.

"We hit it off just like that," Carol later recalled. "We talked and laughed for hours. It was a wonderful night. I look back now and think maybe it was love at first sight. Dan was so interested in me. He seemed so intelligent and I was really flattered. There was a group of Renaissance Party and Klan people at the table. But he singled me out. He told me all about the Klan. I was fascinated."

On the following day Carol was even more flattered to receive a long, typewritten letter from Burros, describing the Klan and his own role in it.

"He must have stayed up all night writing it," she said, "and I was impressed. He asked for my phone number and I wrote back, giving him the number. He called me a day later and we saw each other almost constantly after that."

Carol decided to join the Klan and Burros helped her to

pick the name by which she would be known—Carol Lee Deane. Just before her swearing-in, Burros put his Klan robe on her and walked around her, clucking with pleasure.

"He was very excited and happy. So was I," Carol said. "Dan kept saying, Great! I just want to look at you."

By now Carol and Burros were seeing each other every other night. They often met for dinner, either in Yorkville or the Times Square area. Sometimes they visited friends—Dan's friends—most of them Klan members. "He was very nice with children when we visited people," Carol recalled. "Children always seeemd to like him and he would wrestle and push back and forth a little with the boys."

Burros, who at this period was working at the University Club, printing menus and other club material, spent his money freely; he and Carol often traveled by cab. On one cab ride Burros began talking to the Negro driver's neck about the glories of the KKK. The driver looked straight ahead and Carol and Burros laughed and laughed. Burros gave the driver a fifty-cent tip—"He was always so gentlemanly," Carol recalled fondly.

Often they took long walks and Burros would talk about the Klan, about history, about his Army career.

"He loved the Army," Carol said. "He described every one of his parachute jumps and told me about a friend of his who died on one jump. And we talked a lot about insignias and things like that. He was fascinated with the incidental things about a military organization and so was I. I love symbolism. We would talk for hours about insignias and emblems and uniforms."

Burros' first gift to Carol was a black enamel pendant in the form of a Maltese cross.

"I want you to wear this," he said. "I love you."

Carol felt that she and Burros were "as close as two people can be," but he never told her his secret. What he did tell her was that he was German, that he was unhappy at home, that his parents didn't understand him. Carol found Burros "energetic and tireless, artistic, exceptional." He had "a great sense of humor, was so good-natured, and was always at ease."

They talked only tangentially of marriage. "Carol," Burros would say, "things happen fast in wartime." Carol would nod solemnly. They both knew that they were members of an army and it made them feel warm and together.

Chapter Fourteen

The rest of the story of the life and death of Daniel Burros is simply of markers being picked up one by one, easily and inexorably as he must have known they would one day be picked up.

There are recesses unknown in Burros' life, as there are in every man's, but the nature of his torment he drew as clearly in the pattern of his life as any of his drawings of soldiers and gas chambers. He could not abide life nor could he achieve death, by himself. He fled, leaving the markers, so that when they were discovered he could abandon responsibility for himself in the sensation of entrapment, as a punished, weeping child finally abandons himself in his father's binding arms. To stop feeling, to rest at last, he had to be caught. He saw to this.

The man who shouted "Perish Judah," who was a Nazi lieutenant, who published *Kill* and threw himself into the Jewless KKK, who built his life around the destruction of Judaism, painstakingly made sure that one day he would be discovered as a Jew. He courted arrest, which he knew would lead to investigation of his background, and he courted the police. After he was arrested and convicted in the White Castle trial, there were dozens of people in Richmond Hill who knew that the Jewish boy Dan Burros was a racist. And Burros, by the time he had become a minor power in the

Klan, knew that at least one branch of government was aware that he was a Jew. Still, he frequented his old neighborhood, brought his comrades. He lived often with his Jewish parents. He brought Nazi and KKK friends to his doorstep, in a neighborhood where he was known as a Jew and where rabbis stopped him in the street. He was shouting "Perish Judah" but he was also shouting "Find me," and at last he was found.

The secret, of course, was never really total and Burros knew this. His mother and his father knew—knew of his Nazi collections, his association with Rockwell, his arrest, the fetishism of the fringe right that had become the center of his life.

George and Esther Burros were frightened, but every indication is they were frightened not so much of their son but for him. They knew their relatives were revolted by what had happened to Danny. For the Burroses, as for any Jewish family that sees a son become a Jew-hater, only one explanation is remotely possible—the boy is sick. And to any parents, a child sick in the mind is an unending source of guilt, for where did the illness come from?

The lives of the Burroses, and of Esther particularly, seemed to be woven into two mingled patterns, of expiation and protectiveness. He was their son and no matter what he had become they would fight for him, lie for him, even distort their own thinking in a desperate attempt to rationalize what he was doing, because he was their son.

In Goodwin's Department Store, at 164th Street and Jamaica Avenue, in Queens, where Esther worked as a salesclerk to support herself and her husband, the other employees once in a while would ask after Dan; they remembered how proud of him she had been when he was bar-mitzvahed. But in time it came to be understood, nobody knew just why, that "Essie"

Burros did not like to talk much about her personal life, and the questions stopped.

One of the men who worked in the store says that Essie always seemed to have a headache—"like her *neshoma* [soul] hurt."

Esther was a good worker and was known as a good Jew. The store stayed open on Jewish holidays, but she always asked for Rosh Hashanah and Yom Kippur off, always asked well in advance so the store wouldn't find itself shorthanded at the last minute.

At Goodwin's, she was Essie Sunshine Burros and stayed home on the Jewish holidays, but when the moment of confrontation came, when she faced what she thought was a threat to her one son and the life he had created for himself, she lied for him, pleaded for him and even tried to mask herself for him, so that he would not feel that she had endangered his own disguise.

That moment came shortly after a branch of the Government discovered that Daniel Burros was a Jew. It had not been particularly difficult to discover. After he left the Army and began building his life first around Rockwell, then the New York right-fringe, then the Klan, Burros was investigated a number of times by a variety of agencies of the Government. There is no surprise in the fact that his background of Jewishness was uncovered; the only surprise is that it took so long and that, as far as is known, only a few of the many investigative, police, and judicial agencies with which Burros came into contact were ever made aware of the discovery. Coordination was considerably less than efficient.

The agent assigned to do a fairly cursory investigation of a number of rightists had no difficulty tracking down the parents of Daniel Burros—he had always listed them, with their correct address.

For a half hour or so, he talked with the parents of Burros in their kitchen in Queens. They confirmed that they had known of his association with Rockwell, known but not approved of his anti-Semitism, and put it all down vaguely to "politics."

The investigator began talking about the parents' own background—the entire conversation was on the assumption that they were not Jews—and Esther said quite calmly that her name was Erika, that she had been born Erika Schroeder in Germany.

The agent left and in the next few days, as a matter of routine, checked the Burros marriage certificate. There was, of course, no Erika Schroeder listed, but there was an Esther Sunshine and the marriage had been performed by a rabbi.

The agent called the Burros apartment and told Mrs. Burros what he knew. Mrs. Burros became almost hysterical over the telephone: "Forget it! Don't tell anyone. People will die. Don't put it in your report."

Then, realizing that the report would be made, she made one final plea: "Please tell my son that I didn't tell you this."

Sometime later, the investigator ran across Daniel Burros again and they got into a talk about his mother; once again Burros said she was Erika Schroeder, the German-born Lutheran. The agent shook his head. She was Esther Sunshine Burros, he said—a Jew, like Daniel Burros.

Burros went white and through clenched teeth said he refused to discuss it. "Think it over," the agent said, and left. A few days later they met again and this time Burros complimented him on his detective work.

Where had he found out, Burros asked.

"I want you to know your mother didn't tell me this," said the investigator. "Your mother kept up the charade."

"Thanks for telling me that," Burros said.

The agent looked at him and shook his head—no thanks necessary.

"I'm telling you this not to make you feel better, but because I feel your parents have enough trouble as it is."

Then Burros boasted a bit—about how well he had kept the secret, how he had all kinds of forged identification papers and how he never looked like a Jew anyway.

It was not the agent's business to get into a political or philosophical discussion with Burros, but he did wonder out loud what Burros imagined would have happened to him if Nazi Germany had won the war or invaded the United States—wouldn't he have wound up in a gas chamber? And just suppose he had been old enough to fight—would he have fought the invader?

"I would have joined the *Wehrmacht* or have been an undercover agent for them," Burros said. "I would be a big shot."

But suppose the Nazis had found out he was a Jew?

"There were some good Nazis who were Jewish," Burros insisted.

George and Esther Burros knew, then, that the secret was not a real secret, and in the last years of his life Daniel Burros lived with the realization that he could be exposed as a Jew. But though it must have nagged at him, he seemed to have buried this realization deep in his mind, because he never changed his ways or his habits or attempted to take up a new disguise.

The fact is, however, that the secret was never disclosed by the few Government people who knew about it. It is likely that more than one agency was informed, but many others never knew until the end.

The secret was not disclosed for several reasons. It might have uncovered the sources and methods of inquiry. And all investigative groups prefer to keep knowledge of their subjects to themselves unless there is a specific purpose to be gained from revealing what they know to the people under investigation. Since Burros was one of the substantial number of racists who informed to the police whenever feuds within the parties and splinter groups moved them to anger, there was nothing to be gained by a disclosure that would have blown him out of the racist movement. The investigative branches apparently concluded that there was more to be gained by keeping close watch on Burros and talking to him than by driving him out of his camouflage.

But the markers were all there, waiting.

Chapter Fifteen

In the end, when all the markers were collected, they were placed quite gently before Daniel Burros by a reporter for *The New York Times,* who had never heard of him until six days before, and who lives in the belief of the immediacy and clarity of the word of God. The reporter heard Daniel Burros say, "I will be ruined," heard him say, "I will kill you," and then he put aside his pencil and notebook. He talked then to Burros of the words in the Bible that meant more to the reporter than the face of death: "It is appointed unto men once to die, but after this the judgment." That was on Friday, October 29, 1965.

On October 19, Burros picked up Carol at work and they walked along Broadway toward Times Square, talking about where they would eat that night. As they passed a newspaper kiosk, Carol's eye was caught by the word "Klan" in a headline of the *New York Journal-American.*

Dan bought a paper, walked a few paces reading, and then stopped short at the sight of his own name. The House Committee on Un-American Activities was hearing testimony from Robert M. Shelton, Imperial Wizard, and had released a list of "prominent Klansmen." The list included the name of Daniel Burros. (Burros had come to the committee's attention by attending a meeting of the United Klans of America at Rockwell, North Carolina, on August 22.)

Burros trembled with excitement. "This is terrible. My mother reads the *Journal-American* every day. I could lose my job." He rushed back to the newsstand, bought a half-dozen more copies of the paper, and then they took a taxi to the Brauhaus on East 86th Street in Yorkville. Burros was tense and worried but at the same time seemed rather elated.

Carol was upset and ordered a martini, but Burros would not drink. He told Carol this was a case for self-discipline and self-denial. But he ordered a steak dinner. "Since this is my last meal," he said jokingly, "I'm going to enjoy it." During the meal, however, he kept talking about how upset his mother would be and how he would probably lose his job.

Finally, he got up to leave.

"I have to go home, Carol," he said. "I dread it. My mother will start crying again." He added, "I'm going to work tomorrow as if nothing had happened."

The next day when Burros reported for work at the University Club he was summarily dismissed. Word went out among the northern Klansmen that the heat was on and that the leaders should disappear to avoid the summonses that were out for them. Rotella made immediately for Frankhouser's house in Reading and Burros joined him there on October 22. The Klansmen assumed, correctly, that the federal marshals would try to serve them at their residences but would not look much farther.

A story in *The New York Times* the next morning started the process of picking up the markers. *The New York Times* front-page story from Washington was mostly about Shelton and merely listed Burros as one of the Klansmen named as a leader by the House Committee. The Washington story was followed by a four-paragraph "shirttail" from New York, outlining the information on Burros collected from the *Times'* morgue—that he had been active in the National Renaissance Party, had been arrested in connection with the White Castle case and convicted. The shirttail was written simply as part of newspaper custom, to add to an out-of-town story details that might be of local interest.

That brief shirttail was read by a man in one of the governmental agencies who knew that the Nazi Burros was a Jew. He was astonished to learn that Burros had become a KKK leader. He had known of Burros' career as a Nazi and in the Renaissance Party but had convinced himself that Burros would eventually feel remorse because of his Jewishness and leave racist agitation behind him. This man felt that the fact that Burros had gone on to some prominence in the KKK removed any chance of rehabilitation, that Burros had become a danger to American society. He knew that disclosure of Burros' Jewishness would mean eviction from the racist movement and he felt that this goal was of sufficient moral importance for him to take action.

He notified an acquaintance whom he knew was a friend of a *Times* editor. On Friday, October 22, the editor received a letter from the friend, an employee of a Jewish organization, reporting the "fascinating information" that the man identified in the page 28 shirttail as a "KKK leader and Nazi" was born of Jewish parents and had been bar-mitzvahed. The letter contained some names, addresses.

The editor stood up at his desk as he read the letter. He knew that the author of the letter would not send the *Times* on a wild goose chase and knew that if the story outlined were true it was one the *Times* had to investigate immediately. He knew two questions had to be answered. Was Burros in truth a Jew, and if so, how and why did a Jewish boy become a Nazi? The first question took a week to answer;

the second took more than a year and its answer lies still as much in the minds of other men as in the mind of Burros.

The immediate task was to select a reporter to do the job of investigation. The reporter would have to be infinitely dogged, willing to tramp the streets, wait on corners, follow one lead to another to another. He would have to be able to write well and he must have a sense of compassion. The editor selected McCandlish Phillips.

McCandlish Phillips—"Long John" because John is his first name and because he is six feet five inches long—sits in the fourth row of desks in the block-long *Times* news room. In 1965 he was thirty-seven years old, had been on the *Times* staff for thirteen years, and had developed a quite interesting reputation.

He was, for one thing, known as a "writer." All reporters write; a "writer" is simply a reporter who usually can be counted on to write well, to lift a story out of jargon and routine with his own sense of style, his own eye and ear for detail. Phillips' own quite unconscious trademark is a sense of affection for his subject, whatever his subject happens to be. Phillips manages to see and convey whatever is decent and warm about politicians and the enemies of politicians, about conservationists and about people who want to build plants on rivers, about auctioneers and teachers and priests and old people and young hoodlums. If there is something wrong or "bad" to be reported, Phillips reports it but without hectoring and with a perceptible tinge of regret that things must be so.

Phillips is known as a "writer," and he is known as something quite rare in newspapering, as an entirely and deeply religious man, an evangelical, fundamentalist Christian, "born again" in the revelation of Jesus Christ. He keeps a Bible on his desk and turns to it from time to time during the day. He is pleased when others pick it up to read but sometimes suggests that it is not being read with serious intent, and that this is "trifling" with the Bible and really not to be done. He considers that it is his duty to give of himself fully to his job and for the rest to give of himself entirely to the service of Jesus Christ. He will do little writing outside the *Times* because that would be beyond the duty of his job and thus subtract from the time he has to give to Christian service. He does not preach to his fellow-reporters, but he does preach in his spare time and vacation time in churches and meetings. Outside the *Times,* people sometimes ask whether his deeply religious bent does not "interfere" with his reporting—meaning, of course, whether being religious makes him distort stories in some way or makes him incapable of handling certain assignments. The only answer to that is that the editors of the paper, including the nonbelievers among them, have seen no evidence that reading the Bible every day or even preaching from it, is any particular handicap to a reporter. There are editors, indeed, who believe that if having a Bible on the desk has been of any benefit at all to Phillips, the *Times* might be well advised to form a Gideon Society of its own for the benefit of other reporters.

The editor who had received the letter about the Jew who was a Nazi selected Phillips, walked to his desk, sat down, told the reporter what he knew, and joined two lives together.

That was Friday, October 22. Phillips worked the phone, checking some leads contained in the letter, working outward from them, searching the files of the *Times* for other names, other organizations that had been part of Burros' life. An hour or two later he returned to the metropolitan desk, taut with the story he knew he had just outside his reach. Phillips had compiled a list of people and places the *Times* should check at once—schools, the Army, former employers, court records. Telegrams were sent to the Washington bureau of the *Times* asking for help in checking Washington sources, and two young reporters, Steve Roberts and Ralph Blumenthal, were taken off other assignments and put to work doing legwork for Phillips, checking schools and employers.

The heart of the search, of course, was for Burros himself, and Phillips and a photographer, Carl Gossett, set out that afternoon for Queens. They found the Burros nameplate in the old brass mailboxes. Nobody answered the bell, but outside the traffic cop said certainly, he knew the name and as a matter of fact George Burros had just left the house. He had never heard of Daniel Burros.

They waited outside the house where the Q 10 bus stops and the Army recruiting poster swings in the wind. Every now and then somebody would come along and Phillips would say, "Do you know Dan Burros?" A few people did—"I don't know what he does," one man said, "he's in and out all the time, all hours of the day."

It began to get dark, and to rain. Gossett phoned his desk, was told to go home for the night, and before he left, wrapped Phillips in his raincoat. Phillips waited, talked to another neighbor coming home, arms loaded with groceries. "Dan Burros? A very good boy, never destructive or anything."

It was seven thirty when George Burros stepped off the bus. ("He was a stocky thick-necked square-headed man with a round, pale, and lumpish face," Phillips wrote later. "There was a bulbous nose and somewhat pouted cheeks. There was a kind of deadness to his face.")

Phillips told Mr. Burros his name, that he represented the *Times,* that he wanted to reach Dan—"We have a story about Dan and I need to talk to him." Burros said, "I got nothing to say," and rushed into the house.

Phillips had hoped he would be able to wrap up the story

that night, but it was getting past edition time. He called the metropolitan desk from a bar, was told to come back in. He walked back to the Burros house, wrote a note for Dan on yellow newspaper copy paper, slipped it under the apartment door. A neighbor opened the door off the vestibule: "They're a very quiet family. The mother works, the father is sick. You don't hear much from them." Phillips rode back to Times Square by subway.

Nothing much was done over the weekend, but Monday Phillips and his legmen got to work again. For the next four days, the *Times* backtracked on Burros' life. The Nazi and fringe publications with his name on the mastheads were found; so were Nazis and Renaissance Party people who knew him. They were not told why the *Times* was looking for him. The editors and Phillips were convinced that the story of Burros' Jewishness was true, but the only formal piece of evidence they had been able to uncover was the record of his parents' marriage in a Jewish ceremony in the Bronx.

Phillips had sent a telegram to Burros; no answer. The message slipped under the door had not been answered. On Friday the 29th, Phillips set his alarm clock for 5:15 A.M. and headed out on the long train ride from Manhattan's Upper West Side to Queens. At 8 A.M. he got off the train at the elevated platform, walked down the stairs, turned onto Lefferts Boulevard.

As he turned onto Lefferts Boulevard, he saw the man he recognized from photographs as Daniel Burros just about to walk into a barber shop; a few seconds later and he would not have seen him, would have spent the day futilely waiting outside Burros' house and quite probably, since Burros was planning to return to Reading that day, would never have met him at all.

That was 8:02 A.M., by the roof clock on the corner.

Burros was quite civil; he knew Phillips' name from the note and the telegram, said he had been told by the Imperial Wizard not to give press conferences, but that he would talk a while with Phillips. They looked for a place to sit and talk and walked under the elevated until they found a luncheonette, where they slid into a booth. ("He sat opposite me," Phillips later described it, "a round, short sallow young man who looked like a small heap of misery.") Burros had a Coke and Phillips ordered scrambled eggs.

Phillips told Burros what he knew of his background, not mentioning his Jewish heritage. Burros seemed a little surprised at all the detail but rather admiring—"Gee, fantastic," he would say from time to time—and a little pleased.

The two men talked about schools and jobs, and then Phillips asked him how it was he had become a Nazi.

Burros thought, and said he could not remember exactly but did remember that even in elementary school he had been a "right-winger" while the other kids were of the left. In high school, he said, he had had an "Irish Catholic history teacher who was a McCarthyite, a very brilliant guy, and I remember he used to really give it to those liberal kids.

"That fellow, I can't remember what his name was, sort of crystallized it in my mind."

Burros told then about how he began corresponding with right-wing groups in the United States and Germany, came to believe Germany had been misunderstood in its role as the enemy of Communism. He talked about his experiences in the Army in Little Rock during the integration crisis, how white people had to cross lines of soldiers to get to their own homes.

"I could see America was becoming a left-wing police state," he said, and he said he had made up his mind to fight.

He told about his hatred of the Jews and he said that if the "purge" came to the United States it would be more violent in a "wild" country like the United States than in a "civilized and highly cultured" country like Germany.

With some pride, Burros took out his wallet and showed Phillips the United Klans of America card in the plastic window, a card saying he was a "Special Agent of the Invisible Empire."

Phillips told him some more details he had gathered and, again, "Gee, fantastic," Burros said.

Burros looked at his watch a couple of times, said he wanted to catch a bus for Pennsylvania.

"There's one thing about you that does not fit into the picture," Phillips said quietly. "I can't figure it out. Your parents were married by the Reverend Bernard Kallenberg in a Jewish ceremony in the Bronx."

Until that moment, the conversation had been rather relaxed, and Burros entirely amiable. But at that point he leaned forward, stared at Phillips.

"Are you going to print that?" he demanded.

Phillips said it was not in his power to decide not to print it, that the marriage record was on file in the Bronx Supreme Court.

Burros was tight with fury and with fear: "If you publish that I will be ruined! All my friends, all my associations, everything I've lived for for the last seven years will be gone."

Then came the threats—he would kill Phillips, he had a vial of acid in his pocket and would throw it at him, he would get him, he would kill him before he left the luncheonette.

(Phillips, later: "The whole atmosphere of that luncheonette changed. It was not the place I had walked into. There was blackness in it, blackness crowding around me and perplexity within—and fear. All that came with a few short words, but there seemed to be a power of evil in them.")

Phillips did not believe that Burros had the vial of acid. But he looked down at the table, saw the knives, was afraid Burros might seize one. He put a dollar down on the table to pay for the eggs and coffee. Outside, he felt less fearful.

It was time for Phillips to leave, quickly; he had the story in his notebook and the man he was talking to was dangerous. But Phillips stayed, and he talked then to Burros not as a reporter but as a man of compassion trying to reach a man in turmoil in the only way he thought was valid and meaningful.

Phillips said he knew Burros felt trapped, but that he was not irrevocably trapped and that a new, fresh start awaited any man, in Jesus Christ.

They stood alone under the elevated and Phillips said: "If any man be in Christ he is a new creature; old things are passed away, behold all things are become new."

"You're trying to con me," said Burros.

They walked slowly toward the station. Burros talked again of death, and of threats to Phillips. Phillips said, of himself and of Burros:

"It is appointed unto men once to die, but after this the judgment."

"I'll take my chances on that when it comes," said Burros.

Again and again, Burros said he was trapped, and again Phillips said no, that he was trapped by himself and by what he had gotten into, that he was being driven.

"That may be," said Burros, "but I like it and it's not going to change. This is what I like. I like danger. I love excitement."

At the elevated steps, Phillips again pleaded with Burros to "Break the grip of fascism" by calling upon the name of Jesus Christ.

"If you do that, He will take care of the rest."

They shook hands and Phillips mounted the steps, returned

to the office. He found a message from Burros and during the afternoon Burros called three more times, threatening, pleading, once offering to "trade" the story for another. The last call was 3:50 P.M.

"I know I can't stop that story. But I'm going out in a blaze of glory." He would not say how or when but said he would put on a "show" in the Times Building, even if it meant he would "catch some lead."

That afternoon, the *Times* put Phillips under the protection of its security guard, who were to stay with him, accompany him to and from the office. Phillips was eager to run the story that night. But the editor's decision was to hold it, to get one more piece of evidence that Burros himself had been brought up in Jewishness, to go beyond the fact of his parents' Jewish marriage.

The decision was to look for evidence of the bar mitzvah; the original tip to the *Times* about Burros had not said where he had been bar-mitzvahed.

On the map of Queens, the Richmond Hills-Ozone Park area was marked out by an editor. Two men were assigned to visit every synagogue early Saturday morning. One of them was Ralph Blumenthal and the other was Irving Spiegel, known as Pat, a veteran reporter who specializes in covering Jewish affairs for the *Times,* and who was able to combine old-fashioned police-reporter legwork with a knowledge of Yiddish and an instant rapport with the Jews in the synagogues.

At the first synagogue, the rapport was a little too enthusiastic because the two reporters found themselves the ninth and tenth men needed to make up the *minyan*—the quorum for services—and were pressed into duty. The *Times* has an early deadline on Saturdays—copy cannot be processed much after 2 P.M. for the first edition—and the two reporters tried to control their fidgeting as the service went on.

Just before 1 P.M., Spiegel entered the Congregation of the Sons of Israel and he knew he had his evidence. A plaque to Abraham Burros was on the wall. In a matter of minutes, Spiegel had the story of how Daniel Burros used to be seen at the synagogue with his grandfather, found out that he had been bar-mitzvahed at the Congregation Talmud Torah, checked at the Talmud Torah, and at 1:20 P.M. called the metropolitan desk with details to be inserted in Phillips' story. "Pat," said Phillips, "that's pure gold."

The *Times* ran the story about Burros' Jewish background on Sunday, October 31. Five days earlier, on October 26, the House Committee's subpoena for Burros, dated October 14, had been turned over to Deputy United States Marshal Raymond J. Sullivan for serving. He found it in his box at the United States Marshal's office in the concrete and glass Federal Building at 225 Washington Street, in Brooklyn. It was the first Congressional subpoena Sullivan had ever seen and he was impressed—"I really wanted to do this job right."

Sullivan decided to deliver the summons that evening, just before going home. He parked his car in front of the Burros home, knocked on the door. No answer, and Sullivan walked down the stairs, knocked on a neighbor's door, and was told the Burroses were usually home nights.

At about 9:15 P.M. Sullivan returned to the Burros home. The street was empty and quiet. He walked again through the vestibule doors, and up the stairs and knocked on the door.

"Who is it?" a man asked in a hoarse voice.

"Deputy United States Marshal Sullivan. I'm here to see Daniel. I have a subpoena for him."

Through the door:

"He's not here. Why are you coming here? He's out of town."

"Where out of town? Do you know where I can reach him?"

"We don't know. Why are you bothering us? He's not here. Why are you bothering us?"

"Can I come in for a moment, sir?"

"No. Don't bother us. Go away."

"This is a serious matter. I have a Congressional subpoena for Daniel. I must see him."

"Don't bother us. We don't know anything. Please go away."

"I'll leave but I'll be back."

Sullivan reported the incident the next morning to his superior, Chief Deputy Marshal Joseph O. Denson. They decided it would be useless to keep calling at the house but that they would stake out the house and Nazi haunts in Yorkville—beginning Monday, November 1.

Chapter Sixteen

Federal Marshal Sullivan never got the chance to deliver that subpoena because McCandlish Phillips had found the man they were both looking for first. And the reporter from the *Times,* though he did not know it, was able to find him because Burros had come out of hiding in Reading, Pennsylvania, to pick up in New York his beautiful new Kleagle robe, the scarlet satin robe with the green cape and the violet stripes on the sleeves, the beautiful scarlet satin robe, and the lovely scarlet satin cap with the blue tassel.

The day that the House Un-American Activities Committee announced it was subpoenaing Klan leaders, the day that Burros saw his name in the *Journal-American,* the word went out from Klan headquarters to the Klansmen on the Subcommittee's list—disappear. The word was spread in the North by a member of the Klan's Bureau of Investigation, its security arm, and the instructions to Burros, Rotella, and about four other subpoenaed Klansmen were to hide out at a place known to every government agent as a Klan center—Frankhouser's home in Reading.

Frankhouser himself at first thought it was an idiotic idea but came to see the point—the logic of the purloined letter; who would think of looking for missing Klansmen at a Klan center? (It turned out that Frankhouser himself was served with a subpoena in his home, that the door to the marshal was opened by Burros. But no other marshal ever came back to serve Burros or the other half-dozen Klansmen who were in the house when Frankhouser accepted his subpoena and who stayed on for almost a week afterward.)

The police of Reading, of course, were keeping an eye on the Frankhouser home, but somehow nobody ever put all the unusual activity at 33 South Fourth Street together with the news of the subpoenas from Washington, and the Klansmen who were Frankhouser's guests had some good laughs about that.

Frankhouser enjoyed a good deal of local notoriety because of his Klan activities, and most people in Reading knew about him. There are about 100,000 people in the town and there are not a great many secrets.

Reading is a small valley town in the southwestern part of the state. Like most small valley towns it seems to exist in reaction to the hills roundabout. When the skies are clear and the hills can be seen plainly, Reading becomes a part of them and takes on a lightness, and space. When the hills fade, under clouds or nightfall, Reading seems cut off and forced back into itself, waiting for the hills to return.

The tone of the town, the way it speaks of itself, is quite deliberately modest. "Hurry on down to Reading," urges an official brochure, but the article that describes its resources and advantages is rather subdued. It lists all the reasons that people might want to see or live in Reading, but then goes on to assure the reader that there is no attempt to "beguile anyone into the belief that in Reading, Pennsylvania, the sun shines brightly each and every day and that in Reading each and every night is filled with 'added glories the day cannot reveal.' "

But Reading does relish its past and there is pride in the way that it turns over its history on its tongue. Reading's past is rooted in the migration of the seventeenth-century farmers from the upper Rhine Valley in Germany who fled the desolation of the Thirty Years War. They moved slowly westward and found what they had been seeking in the soil of Pennsylvania and after them came the Huguenots from Alsace-Lorraine, Mennonites from Switzerland, the Moravians, a few Dutch.

Reading is now a manufacturing town, fifty-fourth ranking among the cities of the United States. It has the largest brick-burning kiln in the world and the largest pretzel-baking plant and some six hundred and fifty other industrial establishments. Not many tourists come to Reading and those who do are directed to the landmarks and special sights—the Schuylkill River, Albright College, and particularly the out-of-town roads traveled by the Amish in their buggies.

Frankhouser's saltbox house, which he inherited from his father, is two blocks from Penn Street, Reading's main street, and only another four blocks from City Hall, where the Reading police occupy the main floor. It is a two-story house, of white shingle, and it is entered through the barber shop where Frankhouser's father in his later years used to cut hair and denounce "kikes" and "niggers."

There are a couple of rooms behind the barber shop, where during that last week in October Frankhouser put up Burros, Rotella, and other Klansmen. A stairway leads to Frankhouser's quarters—a bedroom and a living room. There are rifles hanging on the walls of the living room and there are books and pictures, records and a hi-fi.

Frankhouser enjoyed playing host to Klansmen, but that week things were quite uncomfortable. There were too many people in the house for its size, food was short and dreary, and there was too much coming and going for his taste. Frankhouser was aware that there were a lot of people in Reading who were not fond of him; some months before, while Burros was visiting, a shot came through an open window and the bullet cracked Frankhouser's turtle bowl. He never again felt quite as much at home.

There was a tangible amount of tension in the house that week. The Klansmen told each other how hard it was to be a soldier in the right wing, that you had to be good and strong to put up with all the pressures and the way the cops and the Feds harassed you, the way cars followed you, and all. Sometimes it was all fun, they told each other, but when it kept up day after day and you had to hide out, where was the fun of it?

Burros was particularly nervous. He paced up and down in the living room and once said: "God, Roy, if I don't get a rest, I'm going to crack up. I got to get away."

The need to face every test was very much on Burros' mind. He kept saying that no matter how tired you were, man, you couldn't flinch, you had to face up or you couldn't live with yourself.

One night that week Frankhouser and Burros walked to the Peoples' Drug Store, on Penn Street between Seventh and Eighth Streets, where Frankhouser wanted to buy some film. From down the block they saw a group of Negroes near the drugstore and hesitated. As Frankhouser remembers it:

"Dan said to me: 'Are you still going to go in there and get your film?'

"I said, 'Well, Dan, I don't know. I'd better, because if I turn away this time then the next time I'm liable to turn away and it won't be easier, if you know what I mean.' I know what I am and I know what I'm not. I know that I can get scared like anyone else and there's no need trying to bluff yourself. I've been through the mill.

"And he said, 'Well, Roy, I don't know if it's worth it. This time, we just might as well pass it up.'

"I said, 'I don't know if that's common sense, if we're getting smart or if we're getting scared.'

"He said, 'Well, I don't know either, but if I think right, maybe we are getting scared. We better go in there.'

"So I said, 'Yeah, I guess you're right,' and I was thinking 'Jesus, I was hoping he could talk me out of going,' but he was probably hoping I would talk him out of it.

"Well, we went in and the niggers cleared out. They said, 'Man, it's the Ku Klux Klan, oh, man,' and I said, 'Excuse me, gentlemen,' and we went in.

"Then he said, 'Don't ever say gentlemen to them,' and I said, 'Look, Dan, I'm going to say gentlemen to them just to bug them so that they know I'm not afraid of them.' "

Frankhouser made his purchase and on the way out a Negro standing near the door said, "Man, he really thinks he's something, that Ku Klux man and that fat fellow alongside of him."

Burros and Frankhouser started walking away and a group of Negroes, about eight, followed them. Frankhouser says:

"By the time we got to Third there were about fourteen niggers, excuse me, colored folk, following behind. I had a gas gun. It's a pretty potent thing."

Frankhouser wheeled around, pretending to be about to shoot the gun and the Negroes scattered and ran. Burros and Frankhouser started to run in the other direction and rushed into the Berkshire News and Book Store on Fifth Street. They hid in the back while the group of Negroes searched the street for them.

"We were scared, man," Frankhouser says. "I said, 'Well, Dan, I don't care whether you admit it or not but, man, that's murder out there. I lost one eye, man, and two patches ain't going to make it.' He said, 'Well, I think you're right, man.' "

The two men ran out of the bookstore, ran all the way home. Burros was furious at himself.

"I ran from them, I ran from them," he shouted. "This is impossible."

Burros grabbed a carbine that Frankhouser kept in the house, stuck a thirty-shot magazine in it, and taped another magazine onto the gun.

"I'm going out and kill them," he shouted to the frightened Frankhouser.

"I've had enough trouble in this town, Dan," Frankhouser shouted back. "Put that damn carbine down or there's going to be murder. Good God, we'll all get the chair. Shoot them sometime when there's nobody around, or come into town and wipe them out, but don't do it when I'm here. Not now, not today, this will ruin the Klan, ruin everything, it means the chair."

Dan kept shouting: "We ran, we ran, we ran and ran," but he put away the gun and sank into a chair, trembling.

The days passed, with nothing much to do but talk. Klansmen came and went, but there were four who stayed and were a group within a group—Burros, Frankhouser, Rotella, and Frankhouser's twenty-one-year-old girl friend, Regina Kupizszewski.

They talked about the Klan and about another organization to which Frankhouser belonged—the Minute Men, a loosely organized national group whose members drill and practice gunmanship and squirrel away rifles and ammunition against the day, which they are sure will come, when the Communists will take over. Frankhouser told Burros that they ought to get away from the house, go up to the hills where, he said, the Minute Men had caches of guns, and shoot some bazookas, for relaxation. They also talked about a big Klan rally scheduled for Rising Sun, Maryland, on November 7, and what a ball they would have there.

On Wednesday, October 27, Burros told Frankhouser that he was going back to New York for a day or so. He said he wanted to check his correspondence, see Carol, and most of all pick up his new Kleagle robe for the Rising Sun rally. He had to have that robe, which had arrived shortly before and was at his parents' house.

Burros spent Wednesday night and Thursday night with his parents, and it was on the following Friday morning that McCandlish Phillips stopped him in the street, interviewed him, told him that the *Times* knew his secret and would print it, and offered him salvation through Jesus Christ.

Friday about noon Burros met Carol for lunch. He had telephoned or written to her daily during his stay in Reading but had not told her, according to Carol's later account, where he was staying—he simply referred to his hiding out as his "temporary exile." When he met her, he was carrying a duffle bag full of clothes.

"I have to get right back," he said. "They're after me."

They went to a coffee shop called the Avenue at First Avenue and Forty-second Street. During lunch Burros told Carol he had been interviewed by a *Times* reporter but did not say what the interview was about. He seemed very agitated and Carol attributed his concern to the impending hearings and the fact that his parents were, as he put it, "being harassed by the Feds." But he told her, "The worst thing isn't the subpoena, the worst thing is leaving you." Carol was more convinced than ever that Burros wanted to marry her, and would ask her as soon as the trouble was over. But Burros' only allusion to their future together was, again, his often reiterated phrase, "Things happen fast in wartime."

Burros took Carol back to her office at one o'clock.

"He kissed me good-bye and that was the last time I saw him," she said.

Burros boarded a bus for Reading. At one of the rest stops en route he got off to make his last threatening phone call to Phillips. At about 6 P.M. he returned to the house on South Fourth Street.

Chapter Seventeen

Frankhouser was in the house when Burros knocked at the door Friday evening and so were Regina and Rotella.

Burros put his duffle bag away in his room and joined the others in the living room upstairs. He said nothing at first and then it came out, calmly in the beginning and then in a rush.

At first there were just phrases and threats:

"I'm ruined, I'm finished, I've got to end it all. I'm going to go down and blow up the House Committee. I'm going to blow up *The New York Times*."

For a while, as he paced up and down in the living room, he would not answer any questions as to what was bothering him. Then he said he had been interviewed by a *Times* reporter.

"I met a reporter and he dug it up. I admire the man, he's brilliant. He's researched me beyond belief. He found out something that I just can't live with."

Rotella remembers him saying that the "secret" that Phillips had found out was that he was an anti-Christian Odinist, that this would smear the Klan and destroy him. Over and over, he said he had to kill Phillips, had to kill him.

Frankhouser remembers him saying that the next day, Saturday, he was going to check the paper, and "If it happens, I wish you would give me a machine gun, or a couple of grenades and I'm going to do it. I want to go back and blow up *The New York Times*."

At one point he thumped his head and said, "I'm going to have to put a hole through it."

Then he said he was going to kill the President and this terrified Frankhouser. He offered to kill anybody Frankhouser would name—"Just give me their address and I'll go stick up a cabdriver and make him take me there and get the job done."

Frankhouser and Rotella kept trying to calm him down and at one point Frankhouser insisted that Burros turn over a nickel-plated pistol he had been carrying. Frankhouser locked it up in a gun cabinet in his bedroom and then went back to try to pacify Burros.

"All right, listen, Dan," Frankhouser said, "you've got to stop talking this way. Let's cut this violent talk out. We'll become nihilists if we keep talking like this. Violence and violence and violence begets violence. We've got to think in terms of political action."

"No, Roy, this has nothing to do with the military or anything. This has nothing to do with it. This is a matter of leaving the stage at the right time. That's all there is to it."

"No, you're wrong."

Burros thought, and said, "Well, maybe I'm wrong. Maybe tomorrow the paper won't say anything and I'll be clean. You know, man, I want to live." But again he thumped his head: "I'm going to have to put a hole through it."

Frankhouser and Burros left at one point to get a bite at a diner and then returned to the house. Rotella also went out to eat with Burros sometime during the night and they strolled around town while he tried to quiet Burros. Burros kept talking about blowing up the *Times* and Rotella kept advising him that a more practical way of getting at the paper would be to make a speech denouncing it at the Rising Sun rally on November 7. They walked back to the house and there was a "bull session" among Burros, Frankhouser, Rotella, Regina, and several visitors, and everybody went to bed about midnight.

Burros set his alarm clock for 8 A.M. He pulled on his clothes and, accompanied by Rotella, trotted to a newsstand a few blocks away.

"We picked up the *Times* and there was nothing in it about Dan," Rotella says. "So I started to laugh it off, but Dan said, 'Well, maybe tomorrow.' And he was disappointed."

Rotella believed the story had been squashed, whatever it was, because the *Times* didn't think it important enough to print. (The *Times,* of course, was holding the story to get more information about Burros, particularly his bar mitzvah.)

To Frankhouser, Burros seemed jubilant about the fact that the *Times* had not printed a story. He bounded back into the house with Rotella and said they had had "a wonderful breakfast, nothing in the paper, tremendous. I bought that reporter out."

But as the day wore on Burros began to fret again and began to worry that the *Times* had not, after all, been "bought" or frightened.

The rest of Saturday was spent talking about Klan affairs. There were, according to Rotella, a couple of other men in the house during the day, and at one point Regina was sent out of the room to give the men privacy in their shoptalk.

One of the men in the house was a German called Hans. Hans was not a formal Klan member, but was accepted as a believer. He claimed to have been a member of the Hitler Youth, but Burros used to tease him about his stinginess and liked to say that he wasn't really a German but a Jew.

On Saturday afternoon there was a kind of Klan meeting in the house and Burros got out his new red robe. Everybody else sat in regular clothes, but nobody commented on Burros' regalia.

That evening, as Frankhouser and Burros were about to go out to dinner, Burros said: "Roy! I am not going to go unless you give me a gun."

"Well, Dan, I don't like the idea of giving you a gun unless you promise to stop this talk."

"It's for my own protection. You remember those niggers the other week?"

Frankhouser gave him a .32 caliber pistol and they walked out of town to the Riverside Restaurant for a fish dinner.

On the way back, Burros turned gloomy again.

"If it's in the paper tomorrow, it's just got to be done. You tell me what you want me to do. I'll do anything you want."

"There's nothing I want you to do. What is it, man? I don't even care if you are Jewish."

Burros did not react at all to that and Frankhouser thought it must be something else that the *Times* knew—perhaps Burros was a homosexual or had a criminal record.

Burros kept walking and muttering. "Unless I do it. It's got to be done. Oh, I hate to do it."

But that night there was a bit of merriment that convinced Frankhouser that the crisis had passed. Rotella was the butt of jokes about his feet, which the others claimed gave off a powerful odor, and somehow they all got to laughing about it that Saturday night.

Before they went to bed, Burros said to Frankhouser that they should keep some guns handy. He reminded Frankhouser about the sniper's bullet that had shattered the turtle bowl. More recently, there had been another scare—a truckload of Negroes and Puerto Ricans suddenly stopped near the house. The neighbors were frightened and called the police, while the Klansmen rushed to get guns. It turned out that the truck had simply broken down, but it made everybody nervous. So when Burros suggested keeping guns handy Frankhouser replied:

"Well, Dan, I must admit that we have a right to defend ourselves." He says he locked up all the guns except for one—the .32 caliber revolver that he put on top of a tall maple dresser in the bedroom he shared with Regina.

"If anything breaks loose, scream and I'll be down."

According to Frankhouser, five people slept in the house that night—himself, Burros, Regina, Rotella, and Hans. He says Hans was a salesman and left early Sunday morning, before the alarm woke Burros.

Burros dressed quickly, as he had the morning before, and went out to buy a copy of the *Times.*

Rotella says he was still in bed when Burros returned. He called to Burros, "What's in the paper?"

"I haven't had a chance to look at it," Burros answered, and walked into the bedroom he had been using—a depressing little room, painted orange, with a dingy linoleum floor and a few faded prints hung on the wall.

Rotella got out of bed and walked after him. He saw Burros flip over the paper to the bottom half of the front page. Rotella remembers:

"I was in the same room walking after him when he looked down at the page, and said, 'Oh, my God.' Those are the exact words he said. And I said, 'What's the matter?' and he said, '*The New York Times* says I'm of Jewish origin' or something of that sort.

"I said, 'That's not important; we can talk about it.'

"He said, 'No, never,' and he started to run up the stairs.

I'm pretty tall and I'm a lot bigger, even though he's heavier. I held his arm. He pushed away from me and ran up the stairs. I ran up the stairs after him and he was almost three quarters of the stairs ahead of me and he went up there and demanded the gun."

Frankhouser, upstairs with Regina, had heard the front door slam as Burros returned; a short pause, and then:

"I heard a boom boom boom boom, up the steps, just like a rocket. I said, 'Dan?' "

Burros burst through the door.

"It's got to be done. Where's the gun?"

"What are you talking about? What's got to be done?" asked Frankhouser. Burros had not brought the newspaper with him into the room.

"This is it, Roy; I've got to kill myself."

"No, you can't, man, you're crazy, man. Don't dare do that, don't you try. What good is it?"

"Where in the hell have you taken all the guns?" Burros shouted.

Frankhouser looked quickly around the room to be sure there were no guns in evidence. "Look, I locked up the guns and you're not going to get the guns, so lay off me and stop."

"Roy, so help me God, I'll get that gun one way or the other. It's got to be done, Roy. And I don't care how I do it."

The radio could be heard playing—it was Wagner. Rotella came running up the stairs.

In the small bedroom, Frankhouser, Rotella, and Regina confronted Burros.

"Now, Roy, I love you and I'm not going to hurt you," Burros said, "but get out of my way or I'm going to give you a karate chop. I'm not going to hurt you but I'm going to put you down."

"Well, I'll have to defend myself, but you're not going

to get past me," Frankhouser answered. "I don't know what you have on your mind, but you're not going to get any guns. You're not going to get any guns, so that's all there is to it."

Burros swung at Frankhouser, but deliberately missed. Frankhouser stepped back and Burros' eye fell on the padlocked gun cabinet between the two beds. He began breaking it open with karate chops of his hands and feet. The chops twisted the lock so badly the cabinet door would not open. Another kick missed the cabinet and split the side of the bed. Frankhouser watched in amazement.

"Good God, you're wrecking the house," he said.

"I'm sorry, Roy, but out of my way, I'm getting the carbine."

"Don't get the carbine, man, you don't want the carbine. What do you want?"

"Roy, you know what I want."

Regina began yelling, "Stop him, stop him, Roy, do anything, stop him." Rotella joined in: "You're crazy, what is this?"

Burros kept repeating, "Roy, I got to do it. You better get out of the way." Suddenly he said, "I see my gun over there on the dresser."

"Good God," said Frankhouser.

Burros went for the gun. "Don't move," he said.

"Good God," Frankhouser said again.

Burros took the .32 caliber revolver Frankhouser had left on top of the bureau. He held it to his chest.

"Okay, Dan, I don't know what the hell is coming off, but I don't want anything to do with it," Frankhouser said.

"Roy, long live the white race, God bless you, so long, Gina." Burros backed through the doorway about five feet into the adjoining living room. "Long live the white race," he repeated. "I've got nothing more to live for."

Frankhouser has given a sort of stream of consciousness description of the moments that followed:

"Bang! I said Good God! He shot himself, bang! The first thing that I thought of was that he missed. Because he stood there in amazement. I said Good God. I didn't see a hole or anything. Only later did the hole come in, just burnt material, but I didn't even see the burnt material. I could just see the smoke, the sudden blast, the smoke. He said Man, I missed, and the Wagner's playing and Regina's yelling For God's sake, don't shoot yourself, stop him stop him stop him, Roy. I'm saying For God's sake, no and he went, This will do it and he went bang! When he hit himself, he's dead and Regina was screaming, she was still screaming, Don't let him do it and Stop him, and Frank was standing there saying Good Lord because they heard the shot, of course."

Frankhouser says he jumped down the stairs to the phone on the first floor instead of using the phone in the living room, called the operator for an ambulance, was connected to the police at City Hall, again demanded an ambulance, and went upstairs and said to Regina:

"Yeah, he's dead all right. Brother, I'll tell you. It's going to be rough to explain. He's got two bullet holes in him, one in the heart and one in the head. Ten to one, people are going to say this is murder or everything else and we're going to have to visit down there and talk this over.

"And just about then we heard sirens screaming and the police arrive. I said, Well, I'm going to go down. You better remember everything that you saw and don't deviate, don't make up any prevarications. Tell it as you saw it."

But there was a deviation. Frankhouser and Regina both told the police that Frankhouser had run downstairs after the first shot although he said later that he had witnessed both shots. Rotella, in an interview more than six months later, said that Frankhouser was not "even up there for the second shot."

This is Frankhouser's explanation for the discrepancy:

"At that time the police were . . . I was in a confused state and I didn't want to say, Yes I saw him go down and I stood there in amazement, because . . . well, first of all, I should've, probably, but I just didn't feel like bringing it out that I had to stay around for the last shot. It would have been harder if I didn't see it. Because as I said, I've seen men die but never quite like this. Some of it . . . at that particular time I just wanted to get it over with. I didn't sign any statement or anything because I never sign anything, my legal training has taught me never to sign anything. We took the paraffin test also and there were no traces of powder on us at all."

It was only when police had arrived—they arrived within five minutes—that Frankhouser found out why Burros had killed himself.

The policemen asked, and Frankhouser said he thought that the explanation was in the newspaper. "Let's get a copy of *The New York Times* and find out," he said. He went downstairs and found the *Times* on the floor where Burros had thrown it. "Well, there it is," he said. "This is it, right here. Yeah, that's it. Jewish."

Frankhouser's call was booked in at the City Hall police station at 10:28 A.M. It was received by Desk Sergeant James Priebe, who dispatched a police car and sent out a call for an ambulance from the Junior Fire Company, a volunteer group.

The police record states that a pistol was lying six feet from Burros' right heel and goes on:

"A small hole was visible in the right temple. There was

an eight-inch diameter pool of blood under his head. On the left upper chest two inches above the left nipple was a wound."

Burros was dressed in black chino pants, black shoes, Army-type khaki socks, and a short-sleeved shirt. He wore a black belt with a large belt-buckle carrying the initials CSA, for Confederate States Army. On the body were found a picture of Burros in Klan dress, holding a little girl, the note from Phillips asking for an interview, and the telegram from Phillips, dated October 23. Also found was a membership card of the Federation of American Citizens of German Descent in the United States of America and several Ku Klux Klan cards—one designating him as a Grand Dragon, another as a King Kleagle, and two others identifying him as a member of the Klan Bureau of Investigation and Security Guard of the KKK.

The coroner pronounced Burros dead at 11:41 A.M. and the body was removed to St. Joseph's Hospital.

The deputy coroner, Dr. Michael Austin, issued a certificate of suicide at 2:35 P.M. on November 1, the next day. He did so without waiting for the results of the paraffin test, which were to show no powder marks on the hands of Regina, Frankhouser, or Rotella, but did reveal powder specks on the right hand of Burros. The basic factor in determining the verdict, the *Times* reported from Reading, quoting Detective Lieutenant Walter A. Nawoczenski, head of the Homicide Squad, was the "concise and identical" accounts given to the police by three witnesses to the shooting.

Dr. George P. Desjardins, chief pathologist at St. Joseph's, said later that the first bullet wound ultimately would have been fatal to Burros. Dr. Desjardins, who performed the autopsy, said that although the first wound would have killed Burros, there was enough blood circulating in his body to keep him alive for a few minutes and that this gave him the opportunity to fire the second shot into the temple.

Burros' parents arrived in Reading on Monday. They had been notified through the New York City police and had taken a bus to Philadelphia, but arrived in Philadelphia too late on Sunday to transfer to the Reading bus. They spent the night sitting up in the bus station and the next day took the bus to Reading, where they went to the police station.

Detective Paul J. Goldberg was assigned to drive them to St. Joseph's to identify the body. On the way to the hospital, Mr. Burros said nothing. Mrs. Burros kept saying, "He was such a good boy. He never got into trouble. All the trouble started when he got into the Army."

At the hospital, an attendant pulled the white sheet off Burros' face. The parents looked and Mrs. Burros wept. Then they rode back to City Hall with Detective Goldberg, in silence.

In the police station, a huge high-ceilinged place with an air of littered emptiness, the Burroses said they did not want their son's personal effects—two suitcases with clothes and papers. The money in Burros' wallet—$47.73 cents—was turned over to them. They said they wanted their son cremated. (He later was, without religious service; his ashes are buried in Reading.)

The police drove the parents back to the Franklin Street station, a gloomy old building with four rows of dark brown benches.

Frankhouser had left a message with the police saying he wanted to speak to the parents, but because of a change in shifts the message was not delivered. In the evening, he called again.

"I walked up to the station and they were there," said Frankhouser.

"They were bent over. She was on the bench. He was holding his head. I could see the resemblance to Dan to some degree. She had a hat on and looked very haggard, very very tired and fatigued.

"I walked right up to them. And I said, 'Mrs. Burros, for God's sake, I'm terribly sorry about this. And Mr. Burros, what can I do?'

"I didn't know what to do. What could I do? Bring him back to life? I'm no Christ or anything else. So I said I don't know what I can do to help and we talked and she started crying right away."

Chapter Eighteen

Carol was visiting in Washington that Sunday and had not turned on the radio or TV, which all during the day were repeating the story of the life and death of Daniel Burros. She took a train back to New York at 6 P.M., was delayed almost five hours by a tieup caused by a freight train wreck, and arrived in Pennsylvania Station about 2 A.M. Carol decided to stay overnight in a hotel in New York since she had missed the last train to Huntington, Long Island, and she called her mother from a telephone booth.

Her mother told her the news and Carol staggered out of the phone booth to buy a copy of Monday's *Times;* the story of the suicide was on the front page. She walked across the street to the Hotel New Yorker, took a room, and cried herself to sleep.

McCandlish Phillips was at home with a security guard provided by the *Times;* he had been at home at the *Times'* request, with round-the-clock protection, for four days. A *Times* editor telephoned him at one o'clock Sunday afternoon with word that Burros had shot himself.

"He tried to tell me the news gently, slowly," Phillips later wrote. "I felt sad. I knew that Dan Burros had been caught in a net of evil that had pulled him down to death at twenty-eight. I said, 'What I think we've seen here is the God of Israel acting in judgment.' "

The *Times* editor who had received the letter from a friend in a Jewish agency giving the clues to Burros' Jewish background was attending an opera matinee with his family that Sunday. After the first act he called the metropolitan desk to check on the follow-up to Phillips' story, was told that Burros had shot himself in Reading, and left for the office immediately.

After reading the wire-service copy, the first call he made was to the friend who had sent him the letter. The editor and his friend talked for a while, putting into words their own feelings. Both were unhappy at the thought that they had been instrumental in bringing about the death of another human being. Both felt, though, that Burros had pointed a gun at his own head for years and that it was a matter of time before some person or some event would trip the trigger.

(The *Times* received letters from some readers questioning the decision to run the first piece about Burros. Some were from Nazis and other fringe members, venomously denouncing the newspaper. Others were from readers who believed that the *Times* had been guilty of "invading the privacy" of Daniel Burros in printing the story of his Jewish background. Other readers wrote to praise the *Times* for a public service in examining the background of a man who had become a political personality, if only in a minor way, and had thus presented himself for public scrutiny. There was, on the *Times,* an obvious sense of shock and unhappiness that a story in the paper had been the ostensible cause of a man's suicide, but almost to a man, reporters and editors believed that the decision to print the story had been not only correct but professionally and ethically unavoidable. The feeling was that Burros, by taking a decision to become a political activist, had sacrificed any right to keep private any information that might shed light on his motives and actions. Burros' threats to the *Times* and its reporter were never given consideration as a reason for not printing the story. From the moment that the letter sketching Burros' Jewish background arrived in the office, it was taken for granted by all those who knew about it that a Jew who was a Nazi and had spent his life preaching death to the Jew was a story and a front-page story.)

By Sunday night, almost everybody who had heard of Burros while he lived knew of his death. Ray Sullivan, the Federal deputy marshal who had tried to serve the subpoena on Burros and failed, was one exception. He did not see the story until the next morning, in the *Daily News,* on his way to work by subway.

"I read it," he said later, "and I thought I was lucky not to find him. He could have turned a gun on me."

In the office, Sullivan cut out the *News* story, clipped it to the subpoena. He picked up a square rubber stamp and on the first orange page of the subpoena stamped: "Unable to find defendant . . . . in the Eastern District of the United States." He filled in the name "Daniel Burros" in the blank and dropped the subpoena in the chief deputy's box.

If Burros' secret had been kept, his death by suicide would have been worth only a few paragraphs in most papers, none in many, hardly a mention on the air, and no follow-up. As it was, the drama of the suicide the day after exposure, brought an avalanche of publicity to some of the men associated with him in life—people like Madole, Rockwell, and Frankhouser.

Madole reacted with a long, rambling article in his *National Renaissance Bulletin,* full of capitalized phrases and exclamation marks. He dismissed the theories, rather forlornly advanced by some of Burros' relatives, that Burros had been a "spy" for Jewish organizations, or a Federal plant—neither of which was true. "I WOULD STAKE MY LIFE ON DAN'S COMPLETE AND DEDICATED SINCERITY," Madole wrote. His explanation for the tragedy of Burros was that he "could not tolerate the possibility that he would be completely ostracized by all his former comrades in the struggle to perpetuate White Civilization HENCE A COMPLETELY NOBLE PATRIOT WHOSE HATRED FOR THE JEWS HAD ASSUMED VITRIOLIC PROPORTIONS BECAUSE OF HIS OWN INTIMATE KNOWLEDGE OF THEIR DESTRUCTIVE EFFECT UPON WESTERN CULTURE, WHICH DAN HAD ADOPTED AS HIS OWN, SAW FIT TO BLAST HIMSELF INTO OBLIVION AS FINAL PROOF OF HIS LOYALTY."

The death of Daniel Burros led the *Middletown* (New York) *Times-Herald* to examine the background of its hometown right-winger, Robert Burros, and although no family connection between the two men was found, the paper did uncover the fact that Robert Burros' father was Jewish. Before that story appeared, Robert Burros called the *Times* to say that if only Daniel had told him or Madole the truth he would have been assured that he would not have been ostracized, that there were quite a number of Jews who were faithful fascists.

After the *Times-Herald* story about Robert Burros, the "national officers" of the National Renaissance Party met, voted to retain him as a party member because he had, in Madole's words, "abandoned all mental and spiritual ties with the Jewish Community at the age of thirteen." They voted to retain him as NRP director in Orange County, New York, but to remove him from his post as National Secretary "pending a total investigation." Robert Burros repeatedly asserted and reemphasized his devotion to the cause and said he would prove himself "twenty times" more anti-Semitic than ever.

Rockwell basked for a while in the TV, radio, and press spotlight of Daniel Burros' death. He got his own back against Burros in a subsequent issue of *The Storm Trooper* and so did John Patler, who by that time had returned to the Rockwell fold and was editor of the magazine.

The Storm Trooper printed a picture of Burros in Klan regalia and a map of the United States with the Star of David superimposed upon it.

"With his suicide, Burros ended his miserably sad life of lies," wrote *The Storm Trooper*. "There will be countless explanations as to why Burros killed himself. Was it because of idealism? Honor? His only way out? Insanity?

"Regardless of the reasons the Burros Episode is but one more indication of the madness of the people known as 'Jews.' Although the Jews, as a group, are part of the White Family of People, they are a unique people with a distinct mass affliction of mental disorders that distinguishes them from the rest of the White Family of People. The Jewish masses are afflicted with the symptoms of paranoia: delusions of grandeur, delusions of persecution. The Jews believe themselves to be 'God's Chosen People' and they eternally complain about 'persecution' with increasing frequency.

"Dan Burros was the prototype of this unfortunate Jewish psychosis. It cost him his life."

The Klan meeting at Rising Sun, Maryland, to which Frankhouser and Daniel Burros had been looking forward was held and Burros received in death much more attention than he would have in life.

On the speakers' truck in the cow pasture where the Klansmen came together, there was a black wreath, with Burros' name under it. A cross was burned in honor of Burros and

Matt Murphy, the Alabama Klan lawyer, who had died in a car wreck in August. Speaker after speaker praised Burros as a good American. One of the speakers was Roy Frankhouser.

There were good Jews, Frankhouser said, but too many Jews had become mixed up with the Communists, Socialists, Zionists, and Negroes.

"To the good Jews, we offer our love and respect and understanding." But he said the "good Jews" had better separate themselves from the bad ones, as Burros had done. And he added:

"When the chaos comes in this country then things are going to happen like they did in Germany and then God help the Jew because no one else will."

Across the street from the Burros home, a dozen men in their middle twenties were talking football and having a few beers that Sunday when a *Times* reporter told them of Burros' death; the news spread quickly along the bar.

"Oh, yeah," one man said. "I know the one you mean—the guy with the black trench coat."

"That's right, the guy that got mixed up with Rockwell and that bunch."

"A weirdo, sort of a loner, I guess you'd say."

A young man stepped up to the tavern doorway, beer glass in hand. He looked toward the two-story yellow brick building across the street, where the Burros family lived. He raised his right arm in a mock Nazi salute, chuckled and said: *"Sieg Heil."* Nobody else laughed.

In the weeks that followed, the Burros case was a constant topic of conversation, particularly among Jews. Some of these conversations—self-examinations, really—took place in temples and synagogues at special meetings or seminars. One of them was in Beth Ami Synagogue in Scarsdale and the congregation heard from Rabbi Julius Rosenthal, Dr. Morton M. Hodas, a psychiatrist, and from McCandlish Phillips.

Phillips told the story of his investigation and then he told about his own frightened reaction to the morass of hate literature he had to wade through as part of his inquiry.

"It is a literature wonderfully drenched in Jewish plots: There is the Communist Jewish plot, the Zionist Jewish plot, even the Christian Jewish plot, strange to tell. Wild though it is I found that reading so much of it, so repetitive, so monomaniac, strained my own outlook with suspiciousness for several hours afterward. It was hard for me to kick it. As I looked at other passengers on the subway and in the street, I saw some of them through the distorting lens of these ideas. I don't recall ever having such ideas occupy my mind before."

According to a report of the Scarsdale meeting in *Point of View,* a publication of the Workmen's Circle of the Jewish Labor Committee, "an uneasy current ran through the Jewish audience. If hate literature can arouse such sensations in a patently decent and candid Christian . . . !"

Phillips told of Burros' threats to his life and Dr. Hodas did not discount the danger. But he made it clear that he believed Burros from the beginning was headed not for murder but for suicide:

"Why did he go off on a planned trip to Reading if he intended murder as a way of preventing the report from appearing?

"Why did he remain in his old neighborhood and parents' apartment and thus seem to invite ultimate exposure as a Jew?

"It has earmarks of uncontrollable self-destruction. He may have put himself in a position where he could work up enough rage to destroy the Jew whom he had wanted to kill all along."

Phillips told how he had tried to bring Burros to salvation through Christ.

"Do you believe there might have been any way of approaching him with Judaism?" asked Rabbi Rosenthal.

"I don't believe so," Phillips answered. "To bring him to Judaism, if remotely possible, would have required a *process,* for which there was no possible time, but I have seen Christian conversion come to people in an instant and change their whole lives." ("It had happened to me," Phillips said later.)

The psychiatrist and the rabbi speculated a bit on the causes and reasons, each from his own point of view. Dr. Hodas pointed to bits of evidence, emphasizing they were not real analysis—the fact that Burros was the product of a late marriage, which might have led to a cold father-son relationship. Was Burros punishing his father or collaborating with him, in an elaborate fantasy? Was he acting out of self-hate growing out of childhood unhappiness?

The rabbi recalled the stories of Jewish anti-Semites that spot the history of the Jews, and he talked about *rachmones* (compassion).

"Daniel Burros is dead," he said. "We should try to spare him a little *rachmones* for things which have gone terribly wrong for him as a son, as a Jew, and as a man."

Running through all the talk about the Burros case—the sermons, the seminars, the articles in newspapers and magazines—was a sense of puzzlement. People groped for the answer, to try to say how it was that a Jew born of Jews in a free land could so come to hate what he sprang from that he preferred death to acknowledging it.

Nobody ever found the whole answer because nobody knew it, including Daniel Burros himself. But the bits and pieces of the kaleidoscope can be seen, fitted together.

There was in his life the sense of emptiness and failure growing from the differences between his own vision of himself—strong, handsome, martial—and the reality he saw in others' eyes, a dumpy, faintly hysterical boy nobody took terribly seriously.

He fled from his reality into fantasy and found a mask that would not only hide him but from behind which he could for a while blot out the sight of himself in the world. But the flight was never for even an instant entirely successful for Burros could not lose sight of himself, and he hated himself not only for being but for fleeing, an act of cowardice.

Whatever had been Daniel Burros, the honey on the finger tips of the elders of the congregation, had been destroyed by Daniel Burros—destroyed in the schoolyard of John Adams, in the Army, in the barracks at Arlington. It does not matter where. All that existed was the fantasy and when that was killed, its destruction merely confirmed the end of Daniel Burros.

Because, of course, Daniel Burros had ceased to live long before that Sunday in Reading. The fire of his hatred of himself and his origins had burned up his entire personality, without which no man can live. He had already chosen the slow suicide of self-denial and masquerade. Sunday in Reading simply relieved him of the agony.

About the Authors

ARTHUR GELB was born in New York City in 1924 and received his B.A. from New York University. He joined *The New York Times* in 1944 and has been a member of its staff ever since. He is the *Times* metropolitan editor, and among his previous jobs was that of the paper's chief cultural reporter.

Mr. Gelb is a leading authority on Eugene O'Neill. He has written and lectured extensively on the playwright's life and works. With his wife, Barbara, he wrote *O'Neill,* the definitive biography of the playwright. Mr. Gelb wrote the Yale University award-winning O'Neill exhibition sponsored by the State Department at the Sao Paulo Biennial. Mr. Gelb and his wife are also the authors (with Dr. Salvatore Cutolo) of the book *Bellevue Is My Home.* He has also contributed articles to many periodicals, including *The New York Times Magazine, Esquire, The Saturday Evening Post,* and *Horizon.*

A. M. ROSENTHAL was born in Sault Sainte Marie, Ontario, Canada, in 1922. He joined *The New York Times* staff while a senior at City College. Mr. Rosenthal covered the United Nations for the *Times* from 1946 to 1954. During the next four years he reported from India and neighboring countries. In 1958, Mr. Rosenthal was assigned to Poland, but in November of the following year he was expelled by the Communist government for "probing too deeply" into the internal situation in the country. For this reporting Mr. Rosenthal won a Pulitzer Prize, an Overseas Press Club Award, a Page One Award from the New York Newspaper Guild, a George Polk Memorial Award, and other awards. From 1959 to 1961 he filed dispatches from Geneva, Vienna, the Congo, and Central Africa, moving to Tokyo in 1961. Mr. Rosenthal became the metropolitan editor of the *Times* in 1963, and assistant managing editor on January 1, 1967.

A. M. Rosenthal has contributed more than one hundred articles to *The New York Times Magazine, The Saturday Evening Post, Collier's, Foreign Affairs,* and other periodicals. He is the author of *UN: Record and Prospects* and *Thirty-eight Witnesses.*